FROM

Dedication

Tom Landry was truly one of the great Americans and coaches of our time. Coach Landry was one of very few men who have evoked the respect and admiration of a nation. Behind his stoic expression and trademark profile stood a man full of passion who was able to motivate people to reach their fullest potential. While striving to be the best at whatever he laid his hand to, he remained steadfast in his immovable character and his tremendous faith in God.

This book is dedicated to all coaches, players, team chaplains, and fans who aspire to uphold the ideals and values Coach Landry humbly modeled in his life. He left us with a wonderful legacy of what a *true* disciple of *Christ* looks like.

JIM GRASSI

GUTS GRACE & GLORY

A FOOTBALL DEVOTIONAL

COUNTRYMAN

A Division of Thomas Nelson Publishers
Since 1798

www.thomasnelson.com

THOMAS NELSON
Since 1798

NASHVILLE   MEXICO CITY   RIO DE JANEIRO

Published in Nashville, Tennessee, by Thomas Nelson. Thomas Nelson is a registered trademark of HarperCollins Christian Publishing.

Thomas Nelson titles may be purchased in bulk for educational, business, fund-raising, or sales promotional use. For information, please e-mail SpecialMarkets@ThomasNelson.com.

Unless otherwise noted, Scripture quotations are taken from the HOLY BIBLE: NEW INTERNATIONAL VERSION®. © 1973, 1978, 1984 by Biblica, Inc.™ Used by permission of Zondervan Publishing House. All rights reserved.

Scripture quotations marked NKJV are taken from the NEW KING JAMES VERSION. © 1982 by Thomas Nelson. Used by permission. All rights reserved.

Scripture quotations marked HCSB are taken from the HOLMAN CHRISTIAN STANDARD BIBLE. © 1999, 2000, 2002, 2003 by Broadman and Holman Publishers. All rights reserved.

H. Peterson. © 1993, 1994, 1995, 1996, 2000. Used by permission of NavPress Publishing Group. All rights reserved.

Scripture quotations marked NASB are taken from the NEW AMERICAN STANDARD BIBLE®, © The Lockman Foundation 1960, 1962, 1963, 1968, 1971, 1972, 1973, 1975, 1977, 1995. Used by permission.

Scripture quotations marked NRSV are from the NEW REVISED STANDARD VERSION of the Bible. © 1989 by the Division of Christian Education of the National Council of the Churches of Christ in the U.S.A. All rights reserved.

Scripture quotations marked KJV are from the KING JAMES VERSION of the Bible.

Scripture quotations marked TLB are from *The Living Bible* © 1971. Used by permission of Tyndale House Publishers, Inc., Wheaton, Illinois 60189. All rights reserved.

ISBN 978-0-7180-3193-0 (custom)
ISBN 978-1-4003-2089-9

Printed in The United States of America

14 15 16 17 18 RRD 5 4 3 2 1
www.thomasnelson.com

With Appreciation

Thank you to coaches Steve Mariucci, Jon Gruden, Steve Spagnuolo, Mike Waufle, and Tom Cable and a number of players who contributed to my research on this project. I especially want to recognize my good friend Don Davis, retired NFL linebacker, for helping me make a few of the important cameo contacts. To my faithful partner and wife Louise—you're the greatest. Finally, I wish to commend and thank the very gifted staff at Men's Ministry Catalyst for their patience in allowing me to pursue my passion to share God's Word through projects like this.

A Special Thank You

I especially want to thank Kurt and Brenda Warner for their support of this project. Thanks, Kurt, for your foreword. I hope all our readers will support the fine work of Kurt and Brenda's non-profit organization, *First Things First Foundation*. The foundation helps build recreation centers in children's hospitals, rewarding single parents for achieving the dream of home ownership, and encouraging and assisting special needs individuals. You may contact them at www. kurtwarner.org, One N. First Street, Suite 735, Phoenix, AZ 85004.

Table of Contents

FOREWORD

AM NOT SURE WHERE THE POPULAR ADAGE, "NO GUTS, NO GLORY," ORIGINATED, BUT THEY MUST HAVE HAD THE GAME OF FOOTBALL IN MIND. To stand in the pocket, knowing that a 300-pound man is running full speed at you and that your receiver is not quite open yet, so you have to hold the ball another second—letting the defender get closer and closer, only to let the ball go as you get driven to the turf . . . takes guts. To be a running back who goes back to the huddle over and over again knowing as soon as he gets the ball in his hands, eleven guys are going to try to hit him as hard as they possibly can . . . takes guts. To be a coach that is willing to stand up in front of hundreds of cameras and reporters and tell them that you made a mistake that cost your team a game . . . takes guts.

But what I also know is that where there are guts, glory is not too far behind.

It is that last second of holding the ball, allowing a receiver to get open, that often leads to a touchdown being scored . . . glory. It is also more often on the tenth, fifteenth, or twentieth carry that the running back breaks through the line to nothing but open field in front of him as he runs untouched to the end zone . . . glory. And it is in the admitting of fault that a coach earns the trust of his team to the point that they are willing to follow him anywhere . . . glory.

In the game of football, it is next to impossible to get the glory without having the guts to get knocked down, the guts not to be afraid when things are going badly, and the guts to stand up and admit you were wrong. The ironic thing is that this idea is not unique to the game of football.

The game of life, and especially the Christian life, beckons us with the same call, "No Guts, No Glory"!

As difficult as it is for a quarterback to hold the ball a little longer, knowing he is going to get drilled, it's just as difficult to stand up with integrity and determination when a corrupt world is closing in on you, trying to knock you out. As difficult as it is for a running back to get up over and over again, knowing it's only going to lead to another hit, it's just as difficult to turn the other cheek when offended, even though you know it's going to lead to getting hit on the other side. And as difficult as it is for a coach to admit he called the wrong play at a critical moment in a game, it's just as difficult to go to work or look your family in the eye and, regardless of the consequences, admit that you were the reason for the failure.

Football is not a game for wimps! Life is not a game for wimps! And the Christian life, most definitely, is not a game for wimps!

In this book, Dr. Jim Grassi does a wonderful job of using some great anecdotes from the game of football to demonstrate how glory—on and off the field—hinges on the guts with which one plays.

But what I love about this book is that Jim adds the missing piece to the old adage. He understands the need for guts if you are going to achieve glory, but he also shares with us the most essential component to living with both: grace.

Jim does an outstanding job of putting on display the fact that the lives we lead are never perfect. The quarterback often holds the ball too long, resulting in a sack. The running back, no matter how dependable, sometimes fumbles. The coach who makes mistakes is often fired. And the man or woman who desperately wants to live a blameless life will inevitably stumble and fall. Thus, there is always the need for grace.

I believe that in reading this book you will be entertained, but more importantly you will be inspired and encouraged to seek glory by living your life with guts. Guts that allow us to accept our shortcomings and face the most difficult of circumstances with courage, knowing that because Jesus had the guts to live out His life for us, we have been provided with the grace that will ultimately lead to our living in God's glory!

Don't give up on yourself, others, or life. Seek the values and character Jesus spoke of to His disciples when He said, "But seek first his kingdom and his righteousness, and all these things will be given to you as well" (Matthew 6:33).

KURT WARNER
NFL Super Bowl MVP XXXIV

TO SOME, "JUST DO IT" IS A CATCHY PHRASE FOR A SPORTS APPAREL COMPANY. To Robert Griffin III, that phrase has more meaning and purpose. When it was announced that Robert Griffin III was the 2011 Heisman Trophy winner, Baylor fans erupted in cheers of great joy. The man known as "RG3" is the first Heisman winner in Baylor history. In leading Baylor to its first nine-win season since 1986, RG3 threw passes for a new school record of 3,998 yards and 36 touchdowns. He also rushed for 644 yards with 9 touchdowns. [1]

After ESPN pundits have called him "the Most Interesting Man in College Football." [2] A model student-athlete and an obedient, loyal son, RG3 is one of the truly great stories to come out of football in the past decade.

Robert is the youngest of three children whose parents were both Army officers serving overseas. The discipline and commitment to excellence modeled by his loving parents set the stage for his faith, ideals, and family values and contributed to the development of his great character.

When Robert's dad, Robert II, was suddenly deployed to Iraq on the eve of his well-deserved retirement from the Army, it set in motion a series of events that pushed RG3 to become a great student-athlete. Some people take the lemons life gives them and cry over them—others find a way to make some sweet lemonade, which seemed to be the standard RG3 applied to his father's deployment.

The discipline of working hard and studying well prepared RG3 for the task of leading the Baylor Bears in their quest to become a top-ranked team. Robert's practices and study of the game became a model for other aspiring athletes. It was reported that RG3 probably studied more film than most of the coaches. His dad taught him to deal with the unexpected and to prepare himself fully for the challenges life brings. Many of the drills his father invoked challenged RG3 to think outside the box and develop a calm instinct to alarming situations.

Somehow throughout all of this RG3 endeavors to keep a perspective by pointing to heaven after each touchdown. Unlike some high-profile athletes who forget about others, his work with organizations like Friends for Life, which assists seniors and adults with disabilities, and as a coach for kids associated with the Special Olympics helps Robert remain humble and appreciative of God's blessings on his life.

At a time in our culture when most athletes are trying to compete for time in the spotlight, Robert shines it on God, his family, teammates, and coaches. "[God] gives you a stage to make a difference and not to just talk about yourself, but lift Him up. There are a lot of different types of Christians everywhere, but my biggest thing is it's not our job to judge; it's just our job to go out, praise Him, let people know what He's doing, and let people follow if they want to."

Upon reflecting on his faith RG3 also states, "I praise God, I thank Him for everything. Purposefully, you live every day for Him, and when He gives you the opportunity to speak up for Him or to do something in His name, you do it." [3]

Robert Griffin III is off to a great start with the Washington Redskins as their starting quarterback. In his first NFL game, Griffin led the Redskins to a 40–32 victory over the New Orleans Saints and was named the NFC's "Offensive Player of the Week"—the first time a rookie quarterback had ever received that honor for a debut game. But I'd say he's off to an even greater start in the game of life. I think he knows that bringing honor to

God in whatever you do is a real privilege. You too can be the "player of the week" as a respected husband, dad, mom, friend, coworker, or neighbor. Each day we take in breath we can choose to honor or dishonor the One who gave us life.

Like RG3, when striving to be a disciple of Christ, we must remember three important things:

- Serving Christ in the energy of the flesh alone will bring futility and frustration.

- Whenever the Lord tells you to do something, do it.

- Discipleship means following Christ without being irresponsible in our attitudes or behavior.

GAME PLAN:

1. We all have "a stage to make a difference." It may not be the NFL stage like RG3, but it's our workplaces, communities, families, and churches. What can you do to make a difference for Christ on your stage?

2. Are there things keeping you from making a difference? List them out and then prayerfully ask God to help you remove those obstacles so that you can "just do" what needs to be done.

SUPER BOWL XLI WAS A TREAT FOR MILLIONS OF FOOTBALL FANS AROUND THE GLOBE. Not only because it pitted two great teams against each other in the Indianapolis Colts and the Chicago Bears, but also because it featured two great coaches, Tony Dungy and Lovie Smith, who are deeply committed Christian men. In the years leading up to Super Bowl XLI, Smith had worked under Dungy during his years of coaching the Tampa Bay Buccaneers (Smith was the linebacker coach), and the two had become very close friends. After both left the Buccaneers, they remained friends and routinely communicated about their favorite subjects—the Lord and football.

Both men were proud to be the first African-American coaches to lead teams to the Super Bowl. But, at the end of the game, with the Colts being the victors, Tony Dungy said, "I'm proud to be the first African-American coach to win this. But again, more than anything, Lovie Smith and I are not only African-American but also Christian coaches, showing you can do it the Lord's way. We're more proud of that."

After reading about both of these men, watching the attitudes they each displayed on and off the field, and observed how they've consistently earned respect from the players, coaches, and everyone else who is able to work with them, it's evident to me that they live out their faith in God consistently—even when they lose.

Seeing people in prominent positions actively live out their faith in good times and bad times, prompts me to do some healthy self-evaluation

HE FAKED ME OUT
SO BAD ONE TIME
I GOT A FIFTEEN
YARD PENALTY FOR
GRABBING MY OWN
FACEMASK.

D. D. LEWIS, *former
Dallas Cowboys linebacker,
on Franco Harris*

of how I represent Christ in my day-to-day activities. Am I able to consider the confrontations that I encounter on life's journey as "win-win" situations? It may seem like a strange answer, but as followers of Christ, our answer should be a definite "*Yes!*"

When we actively seek a relationship with God through His Word, willingly accept the role He has for us in a given situation, pray fervently about it, and seek wise counsel regarding the situation, we can expect peace—even after a loss. Because, despite the worldly outcome, when we embrace the concept of a win-win confrontation, we can bring glory and honor to God through our actions and words.

The Lord knows how to rescue godly men from trials.
—2 PETER 2:9

GAME PLAN:

1. Have you experienced a loss recently in your personal or professional life? Ask God to show you how your experience can be used to bring glory to Him.

2. Have you ever observed godly attitudes and actions from someone experiencing a loss? Consider letting that person know what an impact their actions made on you personally.

LONG BEFORE THE SUPERSTARS OF TODAY WERE EVEN BORN,

many players and coaches paved the way for them to excel in one of America's favorite sports. From very obscure beginnings, on November 6, 1869, a half-century before there was an NFL, two teams—from Rutgers and Princeton—played what historians consider the first college football game.

The game resembled a soccer or rugby game more than what we now categorize as football. The rules ordered, for instance, "no throwing or running with the round ball, but it could be batted or dribbled." The game attracted a total of one hundred fans, most of whom probably came more out of curiosity than to support any one team or player.

The rival colleges battled to a Rutgers 6–4 victory. Points were scored one at a time by kicking the ball over the goal line, but not through uprights. More games were played, but frustration soon settled in because of the difficulty associated with the rules. Finally, in 1874, needed changes were made.

Records indicate that the first important American coach was Amos Alonzo Stagg. The excitement of football won Coach Stagg's heart and imagination—he had a true passion for the game and loved to encourage younger players. As a Yale divinity student, he began coaching part-time to help pay his tuition. He coached at Springfield College, Massachusetts, and then moved to the University of Chicago. At the age of seventy-one, he became the head coach for the University of the Pacific in Stockton, California.

Some historians credit Stagg with developing the forward pass, the T-formation, the single and double flanker, the huddle, the shift, the man in motion, the quick kick, the short kickoff, and the short punt formation. He helped invent numerous elements of football gear, including uniform numbers, the tackling dummy, the blocking sled, and the padded goalpost.

Coach Stagg died in 1965 at the age of 102, having won 314 games. Only a few coaches would ever win more, including the legendary Paul (Bear) Bryant from the University of Alabama, Bobby Bowden of Florida State, and Eddie Robinson of Grambling. One of Stagg's disciples, Glenn (Pop) Warner, won 336 games by emphasizing the importance of concentrated practice.

In the 1920s, another progressive coach, John Heisman, for whom the trophy honoring the nation's outstanding college player is named, began marketing football in the same way baseball had been promoted. Coach Heisman expanded football throughout the nation, inspiring rule changes that placed a healthy balance between the offensive and defensive aspects of the game.

It was in the same era that the National Football League was formed to take highly skilled college athletes into the professional arena. Franchises began in cities like Chicago, Green Bay, Cleveland, Cincinnati, Detroit, and Buffalo. Most games were played on dirt fields without much padding or protection for the players. You had to be extra tough to play in this league—most men played both offense and defense, adding to the possibility of sustaining a serious injury.

Without championship games and with poor stadium seating, the unmatched teams of the NFL didn't draw many fans during the dark days of the Depression. Baseball was still king, and this newly developing sport seemed more of a nuisance than something of real spectator value. Even so, as NFL championship contests evolved and players' salaries increased, so did viewership. With more rule changes, better equipment and training programs, faster and more specialized athletes, and the advent of television, folks were able to see and support their favorite team.

With the impending merger of the American Football League (AFL) and the National Football League (NFL), a championship game was scheduled for the two titleholders in 1967 and was called the Supergame. This matchup grew to become the yearly super Sunday event known as the Super Bowl, which quickly became the most watched spectacle in television history. Today hundreds of millions of people around the world watch the two top contenders square off for the honor of being crowned Super Bowl champion.

Unlike the evolution of football, God's plan and purpose for humankind does not change. His love for us is constant and unchanging; His promises to us never waver. Our God is a God of order and reason, and the world He has created shows us that truth. He wishes to communicate deeply with us, His dear children, hoping that we will come to know Him and to make Him known.

GAME PLAN:

1. Take time today and find a quiet place (ideally outdoors). Just listen and observe. Can you see the order and reason of His creation? Spend a few minutes in prayer thanking Him for the beauty He has made around you.

2. Look at James 1:17. How do the good and perfect gifts of God's creation help you see His unchanging nature and count on His promises?

4 ALL GLORY IS FLEETING

MANY PEOPLE ATTRIBUTE THE PHRASE "ALL GLORY IS FLEETING" TO GENERAL GEORGE S. PATTON, BUT IT DIDN'T ORIGINATE WITH HIM. In Roman times, a conquering general was allowed a parade of "triumph" through the streets of Rome. But Caesar ordered that a slave stand next to the general in his chariot and continuously whisper in his ear, "All glory is fleeting."

In the realm of football, as it is played out in front of millions of fans in stadiums and on television screens throughout the living rooms of the world, it seems that "all glory is fleeting" is a phrase unknown by many NFL players. In the Christian community though, it's refreshing and encouraging to watch players come into the game who are willing to truly give the glory to God. One such player has become a primary focus of NFL fans.

One of the most decorated college football players over the last decade, Tim Tebow is now a steady force in the NFL. Much has been written about this young man and his fervent dedication to Jesus Christ. The legacy he left at the University of Florida is one that speaks of integrity and character. To this day, his words and actions, both on and off the field, are consistent. There is no doubt that Tebow lives out his faith well. Now, as he faces the challenges of the NFL, there is a great deal of anticipation as fans watch to see how he will live out his faith in such a bright spotlight.

Tebow's heroics with the Denver Broncos during the 2011 season made a definite impression upon football enthusiasts everywhere. Despite the fact the Broncos traded Tim to the Jets it doesn't take away from the spectacular outcomes associated with many of his performances.

"There is no ego with Tim," said Brian Dawkins, a former teammate and nine-time Pro Bowl free safety. "He wants to work, he wants to learn, asks a lot of questions—not just from the offensive side of the ball, but he's asking me questions; he's trying to learn as much as he can to make himself a better player. And that's always an encouraging sign: to see a young guy who's been a star to come in and be a humble player."

Josh McDaniels, former head coach of the Denver Broncos said this of Tebow:

> [Tim's] confidence affects everybody. We could see it last week at rookie camp. There were a bunch of rookies out there with no confidence, except him. He's got such confidence that he will just not let himself fail. And that quality sometimes is very underrated. There are people with a great deal of God-given ability who are fun to watch, and it's really interesting to see what kind of seasons they'll put together. Then there are guys who will say they won't fail, our team's not going to fail, and they have an "I'm not going to let you down" attitude. And that's what you notice with Tim.

Already Tebow's character and strong work ethic are speaking volumes for him and for his Savior Jesus Christ. According to Tebow, "Football gives me a platform and with that platform comes a responsibility and obligation to make a difference in people's lives." God has truly blessed this young man with physical talent and a desire to use his abilities to glorify and honor Jesus Christ.

Are you using the talents and platform God has given you to boldly proclaim His love? Do you strive to live out a Christlike testimony in front of your coworkers, clients, and customers? I encourage you to dig into God's

Word, meet regularly with other believers, and establish accountability with them that will spur you on to glorify the name of God. And remember, all glory is fleeting for us here on earth, but thankfully we are able to glorify and honor God while we're here as a witness of the grace and mercy He has extended to us.

> *I am not ashamed of the gospel, because it is the power of God for the salvation of everyone who believes: first to the Jew, then for the Gentile. For in the gospel a righteousness from God is revealed, a righteousness that is by faith from first to last, just as it is written: "The righteous will live by faith."*
>
> —ROMANS 1:16–17

GAME PLAN:

1. In spite of success or during failure, are you willing to glorify God?

2. Have you seen this response played out in another person's life? What did that look like? How did others perceive their reaction? Was their reaction a testament to God's awesome faithfulness?

IN OBSERVING GOOD COACHES, IT'S COMMON TO HEAR THEM ENCOURAGE THEIR PLAYERS BY SAYING: "FINISH STRONG!" Those who ultimately find their way to the Pro Bowl are players who know how to finish the play, they are committed to doing what is required until the whistle blows, and they know how to complete the task.

All-Pro receiver Jerry Rice was one such player, setting the standard for future wideouts. To watch him practice was like watching a master craftsman at work. When Rice ran a pattern, he didn't quit until he was standing in the end zone. While most receivers break off their pattern when the coach blows the whistle, he continued running until he had exhausted the defensive back or hit the goal line. Then he would hustle back to the huddle for the next mission.

It did not matter that this took a few extra seconds away from the next play—Rice was determined to finish strong each time. The additional yardage he put on during the course of a two-a-day training camp would strengthen his legs, improve his stamina, and help develop an attitude of commitment. Rice consistently led the league in the YAC (yards after catch) category because he was committed to not giving up after he caught the ball. [4]

Whether playing for a Super Bowl ring or competing in the final game of a relatively unsuccessful season, Rice's philosophy was the same: He planned on finishing strong! He focused on every game—whether or not it had any significance in regard to postseason play.

The words "finish strong" are wise counsel not only for a great athlete but also for all of us with a weary heart. Specifically, we need to keep focused upon the victory that is ours through a personal, trusting relationship with Jesus Christ. The apostle Paul had numerous imprisonments as well as other difficulties that would have worn down most people. His strong determination allowed him to pen these words provided by the Holy Spirit: "I count all things to be loss in view of the surpassing value of knowing Christ Jesus my Lord, for whom I have suffered the loss of all things, and count them but rubbish so that I may gain Christ" (Philippians 3:8 NASB).

No amount of punishment, pressure, doubt, fear, or disbelief was going to take away Paul's victorious moments that would ultimately become steps to success. Paul knew that if he focused upon God instead of his circumstances, he would succeed in being an effective witness for Jesus. How else could a man who had been beaten, left for dead, abandoned, and imprisoned write: "Be anxious for nothing, but in everything by prayer and supplication with thanksgiving let your requests be made known to God. And the peace of God, which surpasses all comprehension, will guard your hearts and your minds in Christ Jesus" (Philippians 4:6–7 NASB).

My friend, the answer is as simple as kicking an extra point: Paul had a fixed focus on his loving, gracious Savior—the attitude of his heart was set on the Lord. He never forgot the lessons learned along the Damascus Road, where he felt God's unconditional love. Paul was committed to the course laid out before him; his target was identified and his purpose resolute.

Our attitude shapes the way we view life. Are you feeling like you want to quit or slow down? Perhaps you need to define your goals and commitments more precisely. Maybe your focus is on your circumstances rather than your Savior. Don't doubt, don't waver, don't change course: "Finish strong!"

Let us throw off everything that hinders and the sin that so easily entangles, and let us run with perseverance the race marked out for us. Let us fix our eyes on Jesus.

—HEBREWS 12:1–2

GAME PLAN:

1. Are you like Paul in keeping your focus on God instead of your circumstances?

2. What are some steps you can take in your life that will help you finish strong?

THE UNDERDOG

WHILE MANY MIGHT HAVE DIFFERING OPIN-IONS AS TO WHAT WAS THE GREATEST comeback victory in NFL history, you won't get much of an argument from those who attended the 1992 playoff game between the Houston Oilers and the Buffalo Bills at Rich Stadium in Buffalo. The Bills had played a miserable half of football and were behind the Oilers with a score of 35–3. If "Dandy" Don Meredith had been announcing the game, he would have broken into his chorus, "Turn out the lights, the party's over."

Things were not going well for the Bills' quarterback, Frank Reich, who was starting his first NFL playoff game. Despite being effective during the regular season, the Bills' offense just couldn't get anything going. As the whistle blew to begin the third quarter, Reich started to think about a song he'd listened to several times the preceding week. In fact, he'd written down the lyrics just that morning. It was "In Christ Alone," written by Shawn Craig and Don Koch and sung by Michael English. While no NFL team had ever come back from a 32-point deficit in a playoff game, his faith and confidence remained strong as he reflected on the words of that inspiring song.

The commentators viewing the game called it "nothing short of a miracle." Frank Reich led the Bills to an overtime victory of 41–38. Despite the media's attention being focused on the remarkable victory, God had other plans for the post-game press conference. Reich pulled out the lyrics from "In Christ Alone" and read to the assembled crowd the words that testified to the great faith and perseverance that he and his teammates demonstrated.

I SAID, "SON, I DON'T UNDERSTAND IT WITH YOU. IS IT IGNORANCE OR APATHY?" HE SAID, "COACH, I DON'T KNOW AND I DON'T CARE."

FRANK LAYDEN,
on a former player

Just a few weeks later, Reich again reviewed the comforting words from this song as he and his teammates picked up the pieces after a crushing 52–17 loss to the Dallas Cowboys in Super Bowl XXVII. This time he had a new insight: "The message I was now hearing was that we can experience victory in all our circumstances through Jesus Christ. He gives us the strength and hope to overcome all odds. Looking back on both the Houston game and the Super Bowl, I realize the circumstances I had to overcome were nothing compared to what so many hurting people face on a daily basis." [5]

Simply put, there is more to life than winning for ourselves. What matters is helping others to win—to win by receiving the grace of Jesus Christ—even if it means slowing down or changing our course to help them do so.

The apostle Paul reminded us, "Do not merely look out for your own personal interests, but also for the interests of others" (Philippians 2:4 NASB). God wants us to have a serious, caring involvement in some of the goals others are concerned about. One way we can do this is by taking our eyes off ourselves and thinking about how we can effectively love, serve, and encourage others.

GAME PLAN:

1. Are you actively involved in helping others achieve their goals? If you're not, I urge you to find a ministry within your church or a parachurch organization where you can directly assist others. Trust me; your life will be blessed through this service!

2. If you're a parent or grandparent, are you regularly spending time with your children or grandchildren, encouraging them or assisting them in activities they're passionate about?

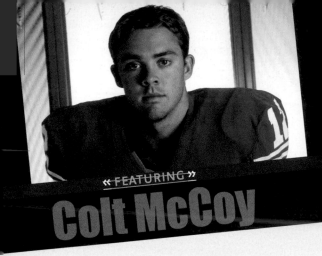

«FEATURING»

Colt McCoy

FAVORITE BIBLE VERSE: COLOSSIANS 3:23

*Whatever you do, work at it with all your heart,
as working for the Lord, not for men.*

After sitting out the 2005 Longhorn season as a redshirt, I was excited to become the starting quarterback for the University of Texas in 2006. My days at Texas were a testimony to how most of us live life. While there are some individuals who are blessed with very few failures or disappointments in life, most of us realize that some days you have great victories and other days you are on your back wondering what in the world just happened.

At this point in my football career, I can say I've experienced the best and the worst the game has to offer. At Texas, I received numerous prestigious awards including the 2006 Valero Alamo Bowl Offensive MVP, 2008 Pacific Life Holiday Bowl Offensive MVP, 2008 Heisman Memorial Trophy Runner-up, and was twice presented with the coveted Walter Camp Award for the best player in college football. As an All-American athlete, I experienced all that comes with success.

And then there is the downside to football. On several occasions I observed highlight videos from the media showing me receiving some of the most vicious hits experienced by a quarterback during those four years I was setting records for the Longhorns. And then there was the Steelers game. As a quarterback, one of the toughest places to call a game is against the Steelers in the hostile environment of Heinz Field in Pittsburgh. What football fan will forget the crushing blow linebacker James Harrison placed on me in the waning moments of that Thursday night, December 8th, game that sent fans and commentators to their knees with pity and concern? Being on your back with a linebacker on you is not my idea of fun.

And so it is in life. Throughout Scripture we see people who had highs and lows. Hebrews 11 chronicles some of the people who saw great heights and suffered great losses in their lives. It tells us of people like Abraham, Isaac, Jacob, Moses, and Gideon. It speaks of how, with their faith, they were able to get off their backs and return to the game of life as stronger people.

My legacy in professional football may not be formed by Hall of Fame statistics, although I will give it my best, but hopefully it will speak more for the guy who routinely took a blow and by the grace of God was, time after time, able to come back and resume the fight. As a follower of Christ, He wants us not to focus on our failures, but to trust God for our successes. That was the message and the grace that Jesus gave Peter in John 21. He told Peter if you really love Me, then quit feeling sorry for yourself, get off your back, and get into the fight of saving souls.

That is my battle cry and the desire of my family. We want to finish well and serve our Lord through whatever platform He gives us.

Pursue peace with all people, and holiness, without which no one will see the Lord.

—HEBREWS 12:14 NKJV

BOBBY BOWDEN STARTED OFF HIS COACHING CAREER BY TAKING A GREAT DEAL OF CRITI-CISM FROM HIS PLAYERS, COLLEGE ALUMNI, SPORTS FANS, AND THE EVER-JUDGMENTAL MEDIA. Some passionate fans even demonstrated their frustration with the new coach by burning him in effigy. Former head coach Bowden struggled through those first few years and learned the importance of character-building seasons.

Bobby Bowden was one of the most successful coaches in college football. He retired with 377 wins and holds the NCAA record for most career wins and bowl wins by a Division I FBS coach. His 1999 Florida State Seminoles became the first college team to begin the year ranked No. 1 in the AP poll and to maintain that ranking throughout the entire season.

Bowden's Christian faith played a big part in his coaching philosophy and was always being tested. Such was the case when Heisman Trophy candidate Peter Warrick was arrested with another teammate for theft from a Tallahassee department store.

Many folks wondered how the great Bowden would handle this difficult situation and if he would dismiss his star player from the team. He struggled to decide upon the appropriate reaction and prayed for guidance.

It was obvious through Bowden's coaching style that he wanted his players to respect their education and develop great character in addition to becoming good athletes. Bowden knew that making poor decisions and falling into temptation could and often would get in the way of a person's career. Our moral values, cultural experience, and parenting have much to do with how we respond to a specific trial. He also hoped that each young person in his program would walk away with a greater understanding and appreciation of Jesus if they experienced His love and grace from a Christian coach.

"I'm just trying to learn from my mistakes and move on," said the grateful Warrick. Undoubtedly Bowden's willingness to give him another chance helped him become a more mature athlete who ultimately led his team to the national championship title, winning the MVP trophy.

Coach Bowden was also aware that each person has the choice of whether he will accept or reject the modeling and mentoring he receives. Despite his best efforts and the encouragement players can receive from Bible study, there are some that just have to learn life the hard way.

Henry Ward Beecher once said, "Troubles are often the tools by which God fashions us for better things." God's Word helps us understand that dealing with life's challenges is what helps produce great character:

> Not only so, but we also rejoice in our sufferings, because we know that suffering produces perseverance; perseverance, character; and character, hope. And hope does not disappoint us, because God has poured out his love into our hearts by the Holy Spirit, whom he has given us. (Romans 5:3–5)

One who undoubtedly had good insight on how to deal with challenges was Jesus' half-brother James, who told us that trials are a part of life and that it is a testing of our faith. We need to persevere, because when we stand the test we will receive the crown of life (eternal peace and great character) that God has promised (James 1:2–12).

When I think about how we should persevere, I'm reminded of the persistence of a dandelion. I have seen construction workers build a driveway that includes two inches of asphalt placed on top of four inches of crushed rock only to have a dandelion seed germinate and push through the entire mass. If there is the tiniest of cracks, that wildflower will struggle through each layer, pushing its roots deeper and deeper to gain strength from the nutrients of the soil so that it can ultimately break through to the life-giving sunlight.

For Christians, our struggles and failures can at times be consuming. But like the dandelion, we are called to root our spirits in God's Word so that we can ultimately push toward the "Sonlight" of Christ, who will fill us with the strength to press on in our work.

At one time or another, we all need grace and forgiveness. And we all need to strive to offer that grace and forgiveness to those around us. After all, it's what Jesus does for each of us. Remember, to extend grace (undeserved favor) to someone is to give one of the most precious gifts you can offer. Don't be afraid to forgive—it might even produce an MVP.

GAME PLAN:

1. Is there someone in your life that you need to extend grace to?

2. Do you need to be the recipient of God's grace and receive His forgiveness in order to persevere?

WHAT'S IN A NAME

IF YOU HANG AROUND FOLKS WHO LIKE TO TALK ABOUT FOOTBALL, IT WON'T TAKE LONG BEFORE THEY WILL MENTION THE NICK-NAMES OF THEIR FAVORITE STARS. To those less passionate about the game and who might observe this dialogue, it's as if some weird charismatic spirit takes over the more animated fans—their language becomes coded and mixed with abbreviations and nonsensical words. Terms like blitz, red dog, cover man, TD, red zone, rollout, under center, screen, and wideout make little sense outside of a football conversation.

Characters who have unique nicknames like the Gipper, Papa Bear, Slingin' Sammy, Golden Boy, Mercury, Bum, Boomer, the Snake, Neon, Mr. Hollywood, Hacksaw, Ickey, Deacon, the Galloping Ghost, Broadway Joe, Whiteshoes, the Zonk, the Fridge, Mean Joe, and Dandy Don are etched in the vivid memory of any fan over fifty years of age.

Each of these names means something to pundits of the game. Most often, it's local sportswriters or teammates that give a person his nickname. Some are earned, while others are a reflection of playing style or persona. You could almost fill a notebook of monikers when listening to ESPN's Chris Berman narrate video clips. His enthusiastic style helps fans identify the person or experience with unusual adjectives and graphic nomenclatures.

But what is the name that is above every name? Recently I was reading a devotional by John MacArthur that helped clarify my thinking on this question. "To be consistent with Scripture, it has to be a name that goes beyond merely distinguishing one person from another," stated MacArthur. "It has to be a name that describes Christ's nature—revealing something of His inner being."

Throughout Scripture, we see Christ distinguished in many ways. Isaiah foretold that He would be known as "Wonderful Counselor, Mighty God, Everlasting Father, Prince of Peace" (Isaiah 9:6). In the New Testament, we see Him called "the bread of life" (John 6:35), "the good shepherd" (John 10:11, 14), "the way and the truth and the life" (John 14:6), and "the resurrection and the life" (John 11:25).

A "nickname" in Scripture indicates the depth of one's relationship to God. The very character of God is such that He requires almost three dozen names to help us understand the various facets of His identity.

When God established His covenant with Abram, He changed his name to "Abraham," which means "father of many nations" (Genesis 17:5). God's special relationship with Jacob required that he be renamed "Israel," meaning "the one who struggles with God" (Genesis 32:28). Jesus took a common fisherman named Simon, who became a "rock" of truth, and renamed him "Peter" (Matthew 16:18).

As the character of Christ grew, God went beyond the common or ordinary in the term that would most describe His only begotten Son. Scores of men in history have been named Jesus. God knew the name "Jesus" alone would not distinguish His precious Son. The only name mentioned in Philippians 2:9–11 that is above every name is "Lord." Paul told us that "God highly exalted Him, and bestowed on Him the name which is above every name, so that at the name of Jesus EVERY KNEE WILL BOW . . . and that every tongue will confess that Jesus Christ is Lord" (NASB).

The name "Lord," *kurios,* is a Greek New Testament term for the description of God as sovereign ruler. It signifies kingship based on power and authority. The name "Lord" as described in the New Testament denotes the God-man Jesus.

Is Jesus the Lord of your life? The greatest "nickname" I've ever heard is *Christian*—a Christian is a disciple of the Lord. To receive Jesus as Lord means that you submit to His sovereignty and authority in your life. As long as He is the playmaker, we need not worry about making the wrong decision.

> *You were washed, you were sanctified, you were justified in the name of the Lord Jesus Christ and by the Spirit of our God.*
> —1 CORINTHIANS 6:11

GAME PLAN:

1. Is Jesus truly the Lord of your life? Is this evident to others around you? Would they give you the nickname of "Christian"?

2. What areas of your life aren't necessarily providing the best evidence of your relationship with God? What are you going to do about it?

3. If Jesus is not the Lord of your life, do you want Him to be? Please go to the end of the book and read God's Game Plan for Life. I pray that you will accept Christ as your Lord and Savior!

TODAY'S QUARTERBACK CAN NO LONGER BE JUST A GREAT ATHLETE; HE MUST ALSO BE A STUDENT OF THE GAME WITH AN EXCELLENT MEMORY. Some teams now have offensive playbooks that boast of 150–170 different plays! Even though players who reach the pro level are already familiar with the basics found in all team playbooks, most NFL teams spend a lot of time in classroom situations, reviewing all the possibilities that exist. In addition to the chalk talks, diagrams, films, and videos, today's classrooms have sophisticated computers that allow the players to see field situations in several dimensions. Welcome to the world of technology.

However, nothing can replace the intelligence and abilities of a great quarterback. Many coaches would say that Peyton Manning is one of the brightest guys to ever play the game. He played 14 seasons with the Indiana Colts, was voted four times as the NFL MVP, and is now continuing his legacy with the Denver Broncos. He has proven to be one of the quickest studies the game has ever seen.

In 2012 Peyton was released by the Colts due to the uncertainty about his neck injury recovery and his age. Within a very short period of time Peyton had to learn an entire new system while becoming connected with the established coaches and teammates in order to create an effective offense. At the speed today's game is played, a quarterback and receiver must precisely coordinate the timing of their moves or there will be disastrous consequences. Peyton's success shows that he has once again proven that he can adapt quickly to difficult situations.

Despite the ability and experience of most quarterbacks, there are precious few who can move to another team and take over the reins

immediately. A dedicated player will usually have to study and analyze for years before his reactions to teammates and new signals become automatic. Peyton's commitment to excellence, even in his preparation for a game, is a well-known trait.

In order for us to develop great character and be consistent in the game of life, we must dedicate ourselves to the preparation and study of the things that will impact us. Most folks will spend about an hour a day listening to the radio, watching television, or reading a newspaper to get caught up on the news. Many attend seminars, retreats, conferences, and workshops to find more efficient and effective ways to complete a task, just as a football player must study the playbook.

HE CARRIES SO MANY TACKLERS WITH HIM, HE'S LISTED IN THE YELLOW PAGES UNDER PUBLIC TRANSPORTATION.

BOB HOPE, *on Marcus Allen*

While all these things will help educate and build self-esteem, the real playbook for life is the Holy Bible. The truths contained in its sixty-six books have not changed in thousands of years. Its message provides answers to the issues challenging us at home, in our place of employment, with our neighbors, and at school. God's Word is knowledge and wisdom that will inform, transform, conform, and reform our very souls. It will renew our minds and renovate our spirits: "Do not conform any longer to the pattern of this world, but be transformed by the renewing of your mind. Then you will be able to test and approve what God's will is—his good, pleasing and perfect will" (Romans 12:2).

How can a young man keep his way pure?
By living according to your word.
—PSALM 119:9

GAME PLAN:

1. Are you spending time daily in God's Word?

2. If not, work hard to find some time to set aside to dive into God's Word. There are so many methods available for Bible study now. Smartphone apps, e-mail devotional programs, and even text message devotionals are widely available. Find a method that works well for you and commit to it—it will change your life!

WHAT LEGACY WOULD YOU LIKE TO LEAVE YOUR FAMILY AND COLLEAGUES AFTER FINISHING YOUR CAREER?

Recognizing that the average NFL player's career lasts about three years, it is important that a player properly embraces and protects each and every moment in order to guard his reputation.

Disgrace and scandals fill the headlines of our daily newspapers. Reporters seem to revel in broadcasting the moral failures of prominent people, especially those connected with professional sports. Hypocrisy prevails as people adopt an attitude of arrogance.

Should a professional football player be expected to maintain a higher standard of conduct than the average worker? Former NFL Commissioner Paul Tagliabue, current NFL Commissioner Roger Goodell, and many head coaches suggest that there is an agreed-upon code of conduct for the professional athlete. However, an epidemic of player arrests for offenses ranging from drunk driving to sexual assault to murder reflects poorly on the league and its teams. Even though discussions about intervention programs and increased discipline continue, teams must find a way to balance the risk by helping players stay within accepted moral bounds.

Dave Wannstedt, former head coach with the Miami Dolphins and now the defensive coordinator for the Buffalo Bills stated, "Character is something that is at the top of our list on draft day."

Peyton Manning, quarterback of the Denver Broncos, had this to say about character: "My dad was a class person on and off the field. That's the person I want to be."

What is character? Pastor Chuck Swindoll reminds us that "character is the moral, ethical, and spiritual undergirding that rests on truth, that reinforces a life, and that resists the temptation to compromise."[6] Character is doing the right thing on purpose, doing the right thing regardless of the consequences.

I've had the privilege of working with a few teams in the area of character development. I regularly ask players to consider their reputation and the legacy they wish to leave when their pro ball days are over. I endeavor to explain the importance of leaving football with a positive image, one that won't soil their family name. A proverb reminds us, "A good name is to be more desired than great wealth" (Proverbs 22:1 NASB). The next generation will not remember the ranking of a player as much as they will recall his attitudes and comments made in front of the camera or how he lived his personal and family life. Character is also the single most consistent quality for success in life.

People—both on the field and off—often compromise their integrity today because they operate from a mindset of following the crowd: they listen more to others than to God. They are more concerned with "being like them" than "being like Him." When Christ delivered His Sermon on the Mount, one purpose was to communicate what is required for godly character (to be like Him). Jesus encouraged His followers to be of good virtue and to act out of a pure heart. If we are to be the "salt of the earth" and the "light of the world" (Matthew 5:13–14), we need to follow Christ's teachings.

I've found that when I take responsibility for my character, the Xs and Os of my life fall into place; when I don't, they fall apart. I hope that when the game of life is over, my friends and family will remember me as a man of good and strong character.

I DIDN'T SEE THE BALL.
I BARELY SAW THE BLUR.

LESTER HAYES,
Former Raider Cornerback,
on a John Elway pass

He has showed you, O man, what is good.
*And what does the L*ORD *require of you?*
To act justly and to love mercy
and to walk humbly with your God.

—MICAH 6:8

GAME PLAN:

1. What does the life you're living say about your character? Is it one of "being like Him"?

2. What are you doing to purposefully encourage and inspire others around you?

WHILE I NEVER HAD THE OPPORTUNITY TO PERSONALLY MEET COACH TOM LANDRY, I KNOW A GREAT DEAL ABOUT HIS CHARACTER AND REPUTATION. We were both a part of the Fellowship of Christian Athletes, and many of my Dallas Theological Seminary friends who knew him well often spoke of his great faith.

There are many who would consider this coach to be one of the most admired and revered men in professional sports. In Bob St. John's book, *Landry: The Legend and the Legacy*, many of Landry's personal character traits, football successes, and spiritual experiences are discussed in detail. The testimonies of several prominent people connected with football help us to understand what made up this successful man. If you desire to have a great legacy, the following attributes—identified by those who knew Landry well—should be placed on the top of your list.

He was the classiest act in coaching . . .
a great coach but a greater man. . . . I loved him for what he
meant in my life and what he meant to the game.
—MIKE DITKA, FORMER CHICAGO BEARS COACH

He taught me to take the heat; just stand up and take it. . . .
That gave me great confidence when I could have lost it.
When he did that, he got me for life. I would have run
through a brick wall for him. He had such patience
and insight into human nature.
—CHARLIE WATERS, FORMER DALLAS COWBOY

*Tom Landry had a decency about him that was
unsurpassed. . . . He did things for the right reasons.
That's what his Christian religion taught him to do . . .
the right thing.*

—ROGER STAUBACH, HALL OF FAME DALLAS COWBOY

*I don't need to be in the Hall of Fame or Ring of Honor to
punctuate my career. What counts . . . more than anything is
that I played eleven years for Coach Tom Landry.
You can't get any more respect than that.*

—DREW PEARSON, FORMER DALLAS COWBOY

*Landry's legacy is one of towering achievements,
modest demeanor, discipline, teamwork, straight talk,
loyalty, commitment, and faith.*

—PAUL TAGLIABUE, FORMER NFL COMMISSIONER

Coach Landry was the best representative the game could offer. From the glory years of contending Super Bowl teams through the dog days at the end of his career, he was consistently a gentleman and a committed man of God. When the team's new owner fired the "world's favorite coach," a seismic shockwave was set off in Dallas. People felt betrayed and abandoned as football lost a great leader and friend.

I believe that a little of America's goodness died with the passing of Tom Landry in February 2000. The coach was once quoted as saying, "As a model for my approach to athletes I think of Abraham, the Old Testament patriarch. His greatness was found in his hospitality to strangers (Genesis 18:1–8), his obedience to God (Genesis 26:5), and the blessing of the Lord upon his family and his life (Genesis 24:1)."

Landry went on to say, "My encouragement to football players is to develop a Christ-like character. I remind them that the greatest honor is not playing in a Super Bowl or being inducted into the Hall of Fame but having their name used to describe God the Father." [7]

Scripture refers to the Lord as "the God of Abraham" (Genesis 26:24 KJV). What an honor! In James 2:23, we see Abraham called "God's friend." There is no greater reward or tribute for a person than to have the God of all creation call him His friend. Abraham's example of love, respect, obedience, faithfulness, and praise should inspire each of us to become known as God's friend. Coach Tom Landry certainly was.

But you, O Israel, my servant, Jacob, whom I have chosen, you descendants of Abraham my friend. . . I have chosen you and not rejected you.

—ISAIAH 41:8–9

GAME PLAN:

1. Are you known among your family, friends, and coworkers as a friend of God? Do they know of your relationship with Him through your words and actions?

2. Have you surrounded yourself with other Christlike men who spur you on to grow deeper in your relationship with Christ?

3. Are you setting aside time during your day to meditate on God's Word and to pray?

⑫ CONFIDENCE

EVERY JANUARY WE FOCUS ON THE CRITICAL PLAYOFF GAMES. We usually see players performing at their very best as they compete for the coveted prize of the championship. I'm convinced that the confidence of the quarterback is a key factor in the outcome of any team's efforts. When a quarterback passes the ball, there are basically four possibilities: a completion, an incompletion, a penalty, or an interception. With those odds, a quarterback needs a great deal of confidence to be successful. If he loses confidence in himself, his offensive line, his coaches, or his receivers, he runs a high risk of failure.

When we look into the significance of this word, we find that *confidence* is a firm belief in one's abilities to accomplish a task. It is feeling certain of, assured of, or reliant upon one's power to succeed.

In his book *Play Football the NFL Way*, Tom Bass stated, "Height and weight may vary considerably from one quarterback to another, but all successful quarterbacks have an inner strength and belief in themselves." To be triumphant, a quarterback needs to bring an air of confidence onto the field and into the huddle. His motivating spirit becomes contagious and is quickly transmitted. Great quarterbacks exude confidence in their team, their coaches, their play-calling abilities, and their God-given skills.

Confidence can be two-sided. When an affirming spirit becomes conceited or arrogant, it becomes a turnoff to the very people we are trying to motivate. As believers in Christ, we need to be confident about our relationship with God, while exuding a compassionate, caring spirit to others.

WE CAN'T RUN. WE CAN'T PASS. WE CAN'T STOP THE RUN. WE CAN'T STOP THE PASS. WE CAN'T KICK. OTHER THAN THAT, WE'RE JUST NOT A VERY GOOD FOOTBALL TEAM RIGHT NOW.

BRUCE COSLET,
Former Offensive Coordinator, Dallas Cowboys

When the apostle Paul was facing the executioner's sword, he did so with an assurance that had sustained him through very trying times. His ministry was full of danger, and yet he wouldn't have had it any other way—he was serving his Lord. Paul knew that through his belief and trust in God, he would eventually find perfect peace. He had confidence and assurance in his Savior.

Let's approach life with a confident spirit, displaying the same attitude Paul wrote about in Philippians 1:3–6:

I thank my God every time I remember you. In all my prayers for all of you, I always pray with joy because of your partnership in the gospel from the first day until now, being *confident* of this, that he who began a good work in you will carry it on to completion until the day of Christ Jesus (emphasis added).

GAME PLAN:

1. Are you seeking your confidence in God or in your own abilities?

2. Pray that God will continue to refine your relationship with Him. Pray that He will give you opportunity to instill confidence into your family, friends, and others in their walk with God too.

I REMEMBER WATCHING THE LONGEST GAME IN NFL HISTORY ON CHRISTMAS DAY 1971. It ran

for 82 minutes and 40 seconds (of game time) before it finally ended with a Garo Yepremian field goal that allowed the Dolphins to win 27–24. I couldn't help but think about the pressure Garo must have felt at that precise moment.

With all the missed opportunities in the game, no one was taking this kick for granted. Whether it's punting or placekicking, a player can quickly become the hero or the scapegoat, depending on where his foot hits the ball. It is mastering that particular contact that allows a player to extend his time in the NFL.

Nothing frustrates coaches more than a kicker who is unpredictable and erratic in his ability to simply kick the pigskin through the uprights. Kickers are a unique breed. Much of what they do is more mental than physical. It is exactly this issue that causes frustration in the head coach.

He watches the kicker make 50- and 60-yard field goals in practice. He reminds his special teams coach to make sure that the kicker warms up and has plenty of time kicking into the net on the sidelines before he enters the game. Finally, the coach shouts words of encouragement to the kicker as he runs onto the field. A positive approach to kicking is as important as physical abilities. If the kicker thinks he'll miss, most likely he will.

There probably will never be a kicker as great as my friend Gary Anderson. I first met Gary at a Pro Athletes Outreach program. After playing several years for the Pittsburgh Steelers and the Philadelphia Eagles, he became a free agent and went to the San Francisco 49ers. (He later went on to play for the Minnesota Vikings and then retired as a Tennessee Titan in

2004.) But it was during a chapel program I was doing for the 49ers that Gary and I realized we shared the same passion for fishing and hunting.

During a subsequent bass fishing trip in the California Delta, I came to really know the heart and passion of this remarkable man of God. Gary's dad, a former pro soccer player who is a pastor and evangelist in Africa, inspired Gary through Bible stories and coaching. With his support Gary developed into a great high school soccer player.

"My folks were missionaries in Durban, South Africa," said Gary. "I played a great deal of soccer there but never even saw a football field until I came 'across the pond' and attended Syracuse University." [8]

Gary was a walk-on who tried out for the football and rugby teams. He didn't even know the fundamental rules of American football, but he impressed the coaches with his kicking style. After playing four years of college ball and earning All-American honors as a senior, he tried out with the Eagles and the Bills. Gary finally signed with the Steelers just before the season began. He went on to play more than twenty years of NFL football, while becoming a four-time Pro Bowl selection.

I remember chatting with him after the 1997 season when the 49ers decided that he probably couldn't kick another year. Gary said, "As long as I feel I can contribute to the game and the good Lord lets me kick—I'm going to kick." It was the next season that he set an NFL record.

Up until 2006, only one field goal kicker had ever had a perfect season—35 attempts and 35 field goals plus 59 PAT (point after touchdown) attempts with 59 successful kicks—and that is Gary Anderson. This was accomplished in 1998 as he was celebrating his thirty-ninth birthday. Over his career, Gary scored 2,434 points—second only to Morten Anderson's record of 2,544 points. One of the reasons for his great success is that Gary never took for granted the unique gift and abilities God gave him. He worked hard at perfecting his trade and never took even an extra point try for granted. His abiding faith and his inspirational approach to the game have helped encourage many younger players and even this old sage.

Placekickers are especially careful in choosing a holder with good hands and a calm spirit. The holder is to the kicker what a reel is to a fishing rod; they must work in perfect harmony in order to complete the job. After taking the snap, a holder must spin the ball so the laces face the goalpost. If the laces are anywhere but straight forward the ball can wobble, reduce in distance, or lose accuracy. The ball is centered exactly to the kicker's preference so that each kick will be placed in the same position relative to the holder's hands. A holder is usually one of the kicker's best and most trusted friends.

The book of Proverbs is full of great advice about the benefits of having a good friend, a buddy you can count on. We all need someone to hold those unique burdens, placing them into proper perspective so we can kick them where they belong—into the hands of a caring and loving God.

GAME PLAN:

1. Do you have such a friend? If not, pray that God will send such a friend into your life.

2. Are you such a friend?

⑭ HUMBLE THYSELF

WISE WORDS FROM THE NEW TESTAMENT REMIND US OF THE IMPORTANCE HUMILITY CAN PLAY IN OUR LIVES: "Humble yourselves in the presence of the Lord, and He will exalt you" (James 4:10 NASB).

After an exciting touchdown run, it is refreshing to see so many professional football players kneel to the ground to celebrate their success with a quiet, reflective moment. It's a real contrast to the vibrant, ego-centered rampages we saw during most of the 1990s.

Backslapping, head-pounding, and high strutting has its place and reward, but blessed are those who acknowledge the success they've achieved without making a mockery of the game. Excessive celebrations often bring unnecessary delay and incur deep resentment and bitter criticism from the opposing team. Finally, in 1998, the league said enough is enough! Let's put the emphasis where it belongs—on good sportsmanship and grateful hearts—instead of on those few players wishing to show off their latest dance moves.

When I reflect upon who God is—how He is so powerful, infinitely holy, sovereign, mighty, majestic, glorious—all I can see is my own sin and how ordinary I am. I'm reminded of the humility Isaiah experienced when confronted with the reality of God Almighty. He ended up cursing himself: "Woe is me, for I am ruined! Because I am a man of unclean lips, and I live among a people of unclean lips; for my eyes have seen the King, the LORD of hosts" (Isaiah 6:5 NASB).

In the New Testament we know the disciples were humbled after Jesus stilled the storm on the Sea of Galilee: "They became very much afraid and said to one another, 'Who then is this, that even the wind and the sea obey Him?'" (Mark 4:41 NASB). If we're humbled before the true God, we'll have the same response as these disciples.

When people face the holy presence of God in their lives, the natural response is to become fearful. But God does not leave us cowering in terror. Scripture tells us that if we are humbled in spirit, knowing that we are saved by grace, we will be sanctified (set apart—freed) and ultimately glorified.

The apostle Paul summarized this in Ephesians 2:4–7:

> But God, being rich in mercy, because of His great love with which He loved us, even when we were dead in our transgressions, made us alive together with Christ (by grace you have been saved), and raised us up with Him, and seated us with Him in the heavenly places in Christ Jesus, so that in the ages to come He might show the surpassing riches of His grace in kindness toward us in Christ Jesus. (NASB)

Dear friend, while respecting the power and might of God, remember His great love and gracious heart. The first step to humility is to understand our sinfulness and ask for forgiveness. Christ showed us humility by becoming a man and living as a servant. Let's humbly serve others then, in a Christlike manner. Next time an athlete takes a moment to give some quiet reflection to God for His goodness, let's give that person an extra hand.

WAITING FOR THE RAMS TO
WIN A SUPER BOWL IS LIKE
LEAVING THE PORCH LIGHT
ON FOR JIMMY HOFFA.

MILTON BERLE

*But be sure to fear the Lord and serve him
faithfully with all your heart; consider what
great things he has done for you.*

—1 SAMUEL 12:24

GAME PLAN:

1. Are there times in your daily
   life when it would be better
   to react with humility rather
   than prideful self-appreciation?

2. How does your humility—or lack of
   it—affect the attitudes of those around
   you?

« FEATURING »

LaDainian (LT) Tomlinson

FAVORITE BIBLE VERSE: PHILIPPIANS 4:13

I can do everything through him who gives me strength.

On June 18, 2012, I announced my retirement to an assembled group of reporters in San Diego, California, just four days shy of my thirty-third birthday. My retirement came as a result of my conscious decision that I was ready to move on to the next phase of my life. Many sports writers have said that I was one of the most powerful running backs to ever play the game. I praise God that I was selected to five Pro Bowls and was an All-Pro five times. I was also fortunate to win two rushing titles, in 2006 and 2007. The statistics tell me that when I retired I was ranked fifth with (13,684) career rushing yards, seventh in all-purpose yards (18,456), second in rushing touchdowns (145), and third in total touchdowns (162). Not bad for "slow." In 2006 I set several records and received numerous honors and awards including the NFL's Most Valuable Player Award and the Associated Press Offensive Player of the Year Award.

I'm often asked the question, "What motivates an athlete? Why do some guys with great talent never reach the plateau that you reached? Could it be great coaching or playing for the right college, or being in the right place at the right time?" I think it's the challenges in life and how one reacts to those challenges that create a certain "drive" and a desire that cannot be artificially manufactured just through hard work, instincts, training camps, and watching game films alone. I guess I had that desire, along with a great faith in God and my teammates, and having those things enabled me to accomplish all I did.

I received a blow early in life, at the tender age of seven years old, when my dad left the family. My mother (Loreane Chappelle) worked as a preacher and encouraged me to be all I could be. Later in life (2006) I again would be devastated when my father (Oliver Tomlinson) and step-brother (Ronald McClain) died in a tragic auto accident. While these events would mentally cripple most people, I used the opportunities to fuel my passion, faith, and work ethic.

If you analyze my life, I was no stranger to challenges in the game of football either. By many pro scouts' reports, I was a power running back who wasn't big enough or strong enough or powerful enough for anyone to take seriously as an NFL power running back. My speed and quickness were initially challenged by several so-called experts. At least, that's what people thought before I showed up at the NFL Scouting Combine and ran the 40-yard dash at a blistering time of 4.36 seconds.

In an article written by John Gennaro on June 25, 2012, he stated, "His (LT's) entire career was an answer to every critic that said that Tomlinson wasn't enough. Not strong enough, not fast enough, not big enough . . . not meant to be one of the league's best RBs of all time. I've heard enough stories and seen enough myself to know how LT became the player that he was. Nobody was smarter about the decisions they made, both on and off the field. Nobody worked harder at their craft (running, blocking, catching, learning the playbook)."

Regarding my retirement from football, I can only say this: I always believe that your later years will be greater than your former years. That's from the Bible. (Job 42:12) I believe in that. And that's how I live my life. I know I'm going to struggle with it—just the competitive part, just being able to go out and let loose. I'm not saying I won't miss the game and that sometimes I won't wake up and wish I was playing. I'm going to go through that. That's natural. But I'm comfortable and happy with my life right now and where it's going.

The Pulpit Commentary on Ecclesiastes suggests a good understanding on what I was endeavoring to share with the press during my retirement announcement. "The beginnings are attended with anxieties and fears as to ultimate success; while from all such the endings are delivered. As no man can foretell what a day may bring forth, or provide against all possible contingencies, no one can calculate with absolute certainty that any scheme of his contriving will attain to success. Man proposes, but God disposes. When, however, success has been attained there is manifestly no further ground or room for apprehension. The beginnings have periods of labor before them; while the endings have all such periods behind them." [9]

Friends, what's most important is not how we start or the challenges life throws at us, but how we finish. With God's help, I hope to finish well as I continue to work with our Touching Lives Foundation and the LaDainian Tomlinson Preparatory Academy, which are designed to help students achieve their dreams of going to college, playing sports, and reducing the problems associated with teenage obesity.

NOT MANY PEOPLE RISE TO THE TOP OF TWO ELITE, HIGHLY COMPETITIVE PROFESSIONS IN THEIR LIFETIME, but that is exactly what three-time Super Bowl champion and three-time NASCAR champion Joe Gibbs has done. When Joe Gibbs left the San Diego Chargers as an assistant coach and became the head coach of the Washington Redskins, his work was cut out for him. Building a championship team with many players who had mediocre to average careers while playing in the NFL was not exactly the kind of head coaching job Joe initially dreamed about.

Because of his drive, decision making, excellent game plans, and preparation, during his first stint in the National Football League, Gibbs coached the Redskins for twelve seasons (1981–1992) and later came back for four more seasons (2004–2008). His great leadership developed teams that contended for ten playoff appearances, including winning three Super Bowl titles: XVII, XXII, and XXVI.

Coach Gibbs instilled accountability, discipline, confidence, and a great work ethic into everyone on the team. His thorough planning and creation of detailed game plans became known throughout the league. Upon reflecting on Coach Gibbs' legacy, Tony Dungy said this: "His (Gibbs') teams were always well prepared, but what struck me was that they seemed to thrive in the toughest environments." In Dungy's analysis of the sixteen years Gibbs was the head coach of the Redskins, he made this comment: "Though, naturally, his goals as a coach included winning football games, winning was never his sole purpose. His purpose was to let everyone around him see how Christ was leading him, and to let people see those Christian principles in action."

Many called Gibbs the best prepared coach in the league. But his decade of dominance in game-winning strategies came at a cost. The cost was experiencing a lot of failures and disappointments. It was through these failures that Joe realized the importance of taking the time and effort to rely upon God's promises found in His Word. In a similar manner, Gibbs had a tough job when it came to motivating his players to trust the coaches' judgment on the game plan and to confidently carry out their respective tasks.

Joe recalls a challenging time getting Joe Theismann to accept the game plan as designed by the coaches. In his excellent book entitled *Game Plan for Life*, Coach Gibbs stated the following:

> Football players have to let their coach be in charge. For many of them, that isn't easy. One of my favorite guys to coach was quarterback Joe Theismann. He had a passion to succeed, but left to his own wishes, he would have liked to call every play. He was the type of player who would rather kneel in the huddle and draw up a play in the dirt than let the coach call the plays.
>
> At our quarterback meeting before my very first preseason game with the Redskins, I outlined an involved game plan that we had been laboring over all week. Then I made the mistake of asking if anybody had anything to add. Well, Theismann had a million suggestions—things he saw, things he wanted to try. Finally I had to interrupt him and remind him of who was in charge, that there was already a game plan in place, and that it was his job to carry it out. [10]

And so it is with our Head Coach—God Almighty. In the game of life, the One who has the best read on our lives is God. He has a game plan for us that is perfect. He has given us the best plan of action ever written—*The Holy Bible*. What God asks us to do is to follow it—to obey His commands and implement His message. Sounds simple, right? But believe me it takes a lifetime of daily recommitting ourselves to make the study of His word a primary goal in our lives.

Plans fail for lack of counsel,
but with many advisers they succeed.
—PROVERBS 15:22

GAME PLAN:

1. Who is calling the plays in your life? You or God?

2. What discipline can you put in place to improve your study of God's Word?

16 OVERCOMING FEAR

TODAY, THERE IS A GREAT DEAL OF TALK ABOUT FEAR. Left in the background of our consciousness are the memories of our concerns for how we would survive Y2K or the outbreak of AIDS. Now our fears have settled upon the problems associated with terrorism and violence. Daily we pick up newspapers and read about the threat of bombings, the hijacking of planes, and violence in faraway places. There is no doubt we live in fearful times.

From meeting many NFL players, I can attest to the fact that these guys seem fearless, but they have much to fear. The size and speed of modern-day players create many opportunities whereby a player could get hurt. Despite the evolution of modern equipment, many players still lose teeth, crack their nose, receive a concussion, break bones, and occasionally suffer a crippling hit or a career-ending injury.

If fear exists in the NFL, it will first be seen among those small, fleet-of-foot cornerbacks who often attempt to take on players weighing a hundred pounds more than they do. The three basic defenses (zone, man-to-man, and prevent) present different problems and risks to the cornerbacks.

The zone defense relies on the cornerbacks taking a specific side of the field, leaving the safeties to cover the middle. Most often the receivers and halfbacks have built up a pretty good head of steam before they reach the cornerbacks' area. This is when some of the most violent collisions occur. In man-to-man coverage, the cornerback is usually bumping the opponent at the line of scrimmage, then running with him, matching the receivers' direction and speed. Finally, the prevent defense is often used late in the second or fourth quarter when additional cornerbacks are placed in the game in order to prevent the bomb.

It has been said that cornerbacks have the toughest job on the field. I don't envy them for a minute. When preparing to face quarterbacks like Manning, Brees, or Brady I would imagine most cornerbacks don't sleep well the night before a game.

Passive or timid players are at risk because they allow the action to come to them instead of being proactive in their assignment. All-Pro safety/cornerback Rod Woodson said, "If you want to be the best cornerback, you have to play like a linebacker too. You have to take on pulling guards and tackles, and you must hit tight ends and running backs." Woodson and other great cornerbacks take the position that fear is something they must control and put out of their mind. They have learned that if fear controls them, they will not be able to perform to their capabilities.

In the same way, it is important not to allow fear to control us in life. Anxiety is a joy-robber that will affect our vibrant witness and worship of God.

What is it that you fear today?

• the loss of job security?

• not being able to pay next month's bills?

• your spouse leaving you for someone else?

• a pending medical test that might bring bad news?

In times of fear, God wants us to trust and obey Him while being confident of His control over every situation. Jesus asked His disciples during a particularly fearful time on a windy sea, "Why are you so afraid? Do you still have no faith?" (Mark 4:40). Let's work on our trust and obedience to an all-powerful God. Attack fear before it attacks you.

HUMILITY IS
ONLY SEVEN DAYS AWAY.

BARRY SWITZER,
Former Dallas Cowboys Coach

"In this world you will have trouble.
But take heart! I have overcome the world."
—JOHN 16:33

GAME PLAN:

1. In your daily walk with God, is there something that scares you?

2. Read Joshua 1:9 and pray that God would give you the courage you need to move beyond your fears and trust Him who is able.

ONE OF THE WISEST MEN TO EVER LIVE, KING SOLOMON, provided some great counsel about the importance of having a good work ethic. The principles taught in his words would resonate with the plan God had for James Brown's life: "Whatever your hand finds to do, do it with all your might, for in the grave, where you are going, there is neither working nor planning nor knowledge nor wisdom" (Ecclesiastes 9:10).

One of the great stories of our day comes from the book *Role of a Lifetime: Reflections on Faith, Family, and Significant Living* by James Brown. The beloved sports commentator, James Brown (JB), had a loving mom and dad who modeled great character for the five children they raised. Their ability to work as a team for the good of the family impacted JB's life. To further support that concept, his high school basketball coach, Mr. Morgan Wootten, challenged him both on and off the court to pursue his dreams with passion and a commitment to excellence.

Regularly his mother and father would remind him, "Son, time is a wasting. Get to your studying and focus on your academics." After playing four years of basketball at Harvard and receiving All-Ivy League honors, James had his shot at the NBA and was twice cut. Though disappointed, he remembered the words of Coach Wootten: "The person who works the hardest usually succeeds the best." And so JB vowed that whatever God gave him as a destiny, he would never let an opportunity go by that he wasn't prepared for.

He didn't seek to become a media star, but it happened—because of the prayers of many, the education he applied, and the hard work he put in by developing the communication and people skills necessary to be a productive citizen.

IF ANYTHING GOES BAD, I DID IT. IF
ANYTHING GOES SEMI-GOOD, THEN
WE DID IT. IF ANYTHING GOES REAL
GOOD, THEN YOU DID IT.

BEAR BRYANT

In a society that is moving toward an entitlement mentality, it is disappointing that so many young people are riding the wave of mediocrity and hopelessness. God's Word reminds all of us, "May the favor of the Lord our God rest upon us; establish the work of our hands for us—yes, establish the work of our hands" (Psalm 90:17).

Whether it's on the football field or basketball court, in the commentator's booth, or in the workplace or the home, we should work hard to make the best of the opportunities we've been given. Many of the football players you have read about in this book didn't necessarily have innate abilities to play the game at the same level they finished their careers. It is through hard work that champions are made and it's by persevering through our trials, pain, and suffering that each of us can succeed. By using our abilities (hands, minds, and passions) as directed by the Holy Spirit, we can build an enduring legacy.

GAME PLAN:

1. What is God's plan for your life? What are your education, experiences, personality, gifts, talents, interests, and skills, and how have they shaped your character? Read Romans 12 and 1 Corinthians 12.

2. How can you use your gifts to serve God and encourage others?

DREW BREES, QUARTERBACK OF THE SUPER BOWL XLIV CHAMPIONS, the New Orleans Saints, has seen his share of setbacks. His "rise to the top" has been wrought with obstacles and yet, through it all his faith in Christ has only deepened since dedicating his life to Christ as a seventeen-year-old young man.

The pastor of his family's church offered up a challenge that he accepted wholeheartedly and ran with. His pastor told the congregation that God was looking for a few good men who were willing to serve Him. Brees was a young man intent on being a leader, desiring purpose and greatness, and this challenge struck a nerve with him.

After deciding to serve the Lord, Drew's road to football stardom began. He set five Big Ten Conference records during his tenure as the quarterback of the Purdue Boilermakers, ultimately earning him the first pick of the second round in the 2001 NFL Draft by the San Diego Chargers. His NFL career didn't take off as quickly as he expected, though, as he divided playing time with San Diego's veteran quarterback, Doug Flutie. However, in 2004 he was given a chance as a starter and seized the moment. That season he earned a trip to the Pro Bowl and led the Chargers to the playoffs. The 2005 season continued in the same manner with Brees setting a career high in passing yards (3,576), but in the last game of the season everything changed. In that game, a hard sack left him with a torn labrum and a partially torn rotator cuff in his throwing shoulder.

After dealing with an injury that was a major setback to his career, Drew not only knew he'd be perceived as "damaged goods" but he also began to question why God had allowed it to happen. But God loves to work out His plan when we are at our weakest point!

While from Drew's vantage point, the timing seemed to be pretty lousy, God's timing was perfect. Hurricane Katrina leveled the city of New Orleans in that same year. The Saints ended the 2005 season with a 3–13 record and were on the hunt for a new quarterback. The Saints picked up Brees for the 2006 season and from that point forward the turnaround was amazing for New Orleans, the Saints, and Drew. The 2006 season ended for the Saints as division champs with a 10–6 record and as NFC runners-up. Moving forward from 2006, the next two seasons were difficult.

However, during those two seasons Drew continued to lead—on and off the field. "Real men of God are always trying to find ways to draw closer to the King. Drew never misses a chapel, team Bible study, or couples' Bible study. His focus is always team-focused instead of Drew-focused. That is the makeup of a true leader," said Heath Evans, former Saints fullback.

Drew himself stated, "Obviously, I have to work to be the best quarterback I can be for the team, but, if there's ever a time when I can help a guy by pulling him aside and talking to him about a route or showing him something in the weight room, I want to do that. But not only with things on the field, but also things in life."

In 2009, the Saints were in full stride and earned their first ever trip to the Super Bowl. They defeated the Indianapolis Colts in Super Bowl XLIV with a score of 31–17 in a victory that came to represent the city of New Orleans' resurgence after being ravaged by Katrina.

Despite sitting the bench for a while and an injury that changed his plans, Drew continued to rely upon the Lord and serve Him. It reminds me of the many tough times King David encountered. As evident in the Psalms, he at times questioned his condition and the situations he found himself in—yet he's listed in Hebrews 11 in a passage commonly referred to as the "heroes of faith."

> *Show me your ways, O LORD,*
> *teach me your paths;*
> *guide me in your truth and teach me,*
> *for you are God my Savior,*
> *and my hope is in you all day long.*
> —PSALM 25:4–5

I pray that these verses penned by King David will be the prayer of your heart daily as you navigate life's journey.

> *Who, then, is the man that fears the LORD?*
> *He will instruct him in the way chosen for him.*
> —PSALM 25:12

GAME PLAN:

1. Resolve to read through the book of Psalms. How does the psalmist deal with trials?

2. Do you know someone who could use the encouragement of a fellow believer in Christ as he or she walks through tough times? Are you willing to pray for that person and offer words of encouragement?

DON DAVIS WAS AN OUTSTANDING STAR FOOTBALL PLAYER FOR THE UNIVERSITY OF KANSAS.

He thought for sure he would be taken in the 1995 NFL Draft only to find that he was passed over. With disappointment came hope. The New York Jets brought him into training camp but cut him soon thereafter. Again there was hope, because the Kansas City Chiefs put him on the practice squad. Unfortunately he was unceremoniously cut and just about gave up on ever having a football career. Don loved the game but found that both his mental focus and physical abilities weren't quite in line with what the coaches were looking for.

After being out of football for three weeks, Don decided to get a job at Foot Locker selling shoes. This was a very humbling experience, as several of the guys he used to play with on the Chiefs would come into the store, spending more money in an hour than he could make in a week. Don found himself really starting to miss football and was determined to rekindle his passion to play the game.

For seven months he dedicated all his time to becoming the best football player he could be. His workouts, focus, and enthusiasm continued to build while training. After another cut by the Chiefs and a year with the Saints, the Tampa Bay Buccaneers signed him. Coach Tony Dungy spoke into Don's life and encouraged him in his performance and faith. That encouragement is what Don needed to ignite his spiritual passion and self-confidence.

After two years with the Buccaneers, Don was signed by the Rams and enjoyed a year of unexplainable blessings and favor. He became a full-time starter for the first time in his career. His team even went to the Super Bowl. Don also saw God's favor on him and was baptized again and really started to become a passionate disciple of Christ. After two years he became a recognized and well-respected player who was signed by the New England Patriots. It was here that he made his statement as a player and follower of Christ. He became a leader in the locker room and through his ministry to those around him.

Although Don now has two Super Bowl rings, there have been many challenges along the way. Only his faith in God has gotten him through those many difficult times and given him the attitude to persevere (Romans 5:3).

And interestingly enough, Don used the fundamental linebacker training he received as a metaphor to remind him about how to live a victorious life. There are three distinctive traits a good linebacker displays in playing that position:

1. **Stance:** Every good linebacker has the proper stance—feet shoulder width apart and your shoulders over the knees and knees over the toes. Spiritually you need to make sure you have the right stance, which starts with the right foundation. (Matthew 7:24–27)

2. **Alignment:** It doesn't matter if a linebacker has a good stance if he is aligned in the wrong gap. Spiritually, once we have a good stance, we need to make sure we have the correct alignment. Who are we lining up with? (Proverbs 13:20; 1 Corinthians 15:33)

3. **Assignment:** If you have the right stance and are aligned properly it will do you no good if you don't know your assignment. Spiritually there are many who have the right stance and are lined up properly, but neglect to study the playbook and therefore don't know the plays. (Colossians 3:16; John 8:31–32)

Don often reminds himself of God's promises and that his first love is to seek God's purpose and plan for his life and family. "For where your treasure is, there your heart will be also" (Matthew 6:21)—and that includes Super Bowl trophies.

Then Jesus said to his disciples, "If anyone would come after me, he must deny himself and take up his cross and follow me."

—MATTHEW 16:24

GAME PLAN:

1. What do the following verses teach you about how you should tackle life's issues: Colossians 3:16, John 8:31–32, and Matthew 8:19–20?

2. What verses would resonate with your story? Make a list of the tests, challenges, disappointments, successes, and answered prayers in your life. What is God showing you about yourself?

20 DAVID AND GOLIATH

AS A YOUNG PERSON GROWING UP IN FLORIDA, Emmitt Smith had a dream of becoming one of the best running backs to ever play football. At six years of age, after watching the Dallas Cowboys play a game on television, Emmitt told his dad that someday he wanted to play for the Cowboys. Like many good fathers, Emmitt's dad affirmed his goal and encouraged the young lad along the way.

Over the years, Emmitt didn't listen to the discouragers who wanted to put him down. There were a few recruiting analysts who opined that he was too small, too slow, and that he couldn't get around the corner.

These opinions seemed to fuel Emmitt's passion, desire, and even anger. Consequently, upon graduating from the University of Florida, he was a unanimous first-team All-American and finished seventh in the Heisman Trophy balloting. Even though he succeeded in college football, some NFL teams still felt he wouldn't make it in the pros. Fortunately, the Dallas Cowboys thought otherwise and picked him up in the first round of the NFL Draft in 1990.

It is reported that Emmitt studied the styles and plays of great running backs like Walter Payton, Barry Sanders, Eric Dickerson, and Gale Sayers to see what made them elusive and deceptive. Smith learned to dart, slither, dive, and follow great blockers—like Daryl Johnston, who would open creases for him to wedge his way forward. Emmitt stated, "God gave me excellent vision, tremendous leg strength, and great balance that allowed me to gain yardage when others might be stopped. Later in life that would even afford me an opportunity to win the 'Dancing with the Stars' competition." [11]

In his excellent Hall of Fame speech Emmitt said, "Whatever achievements I've earned over the course of my life clearly have not been due to luck, but due to the belief and dedication of so many. The values and skills taught by my family, friends, teachers, coaches, and mentors were fundamental to shaping me into the man I am today."

It was about halfway through his professional career that he found himself unsettled and frustrated and discovered the message of the gospel that gave him the faith to walk unafraid in life. [12] Much like the smaller David who faced a bigger Goliath, Emmitt wasn't going to be intimidated by bigger defensive players or deceptive philosophies that would lead him down the wrong path. God became Emmitt's strength and fortress during those times when life was a challenge. And he learned to praise Him for the times when many blessings came his way—and many did.

After playing thirteen seasons with the Dallas Cowboys and two seasons with the Arizona Cardinals, Emmitt finished his career with 18,355 rushing yards and 164 touchdowns. He became the All-Time Rushing Back in the NFL. But the most important record book Smith desires to be in is God's record book of faithful men. Emmitt wants to be remembered for what he does to encourage others the same way that he has been encouraged.

It was for this reason Emmitt and his wife, Pat, created the Pat and Emmitt Smith Charities (PESC) to fund unique educational experiences and enrichment opportunities for underserved children. As the apostle Paul reminded us, "Encourage one another and build each other up" (1 Thessalonians 5:11). And if there is anything we need in America today, it is to be spiritual encouragers of one another.

I WAS SCARED. I THOUGHT DETROIT
WAS GOING TO DRAFT ME. I WAS GOING
TO ASK FOR SO MUCH MONEY THAT
THEY'D HAVE TO PUT ME ON LAYAWAY.

DEION SANDERS

*The LORD is my light and my salvation—
whom shall I fear?
The LORD is the stronghold of my life—
of whom shall I be afraid?*
—PSALM 27:1

GAME PLAN:

1. What are the giants in your life that create confusion, frustration, and challenges?

2. What can you do to help those around you and in your community who are facing giants of their own?

ACCORDING TO *WEBSTER'S*, A WITNESS IS A PERSON WHO SAW AND CAN GIVE A FIRST-HAND ACCOUNT OF SOMETHING. We often think of witnesses in terms of legal actions or courts of law. But in football, the witnesses are the officials, aka the Zebras, who are charged by the NFL to enforce the rules and regulations governing game play.

To the casual observer the officials seem to be part of the landscape, someone to place the ball at the correct spot on the field. If your favorite team receives a questionable penalty, then you see the Zebras as a nuisance or a distraction. Much like the NFL players themselves, professional officials are selected based upon their experience and knowledge of the game. They are chosen because of their unbiased approach to making correct calls during critical situations.

My friend Steve Wilson, a former pastor in Spokane, Washington, is a retired NFL umpire (formerly #29). After interviewing Steve, my perspective of officiating changed drastically. Now I'm extremely impressed with the depth of understanding and anticipation an NFL official must have to be effective.

I learned that each official has specific tasks and responsibilities associated with his position. Being in the right spot at the right time is critical to good play-calling and to one's own survival. If a Zebra happens to daydream on a play where the tight end is crossing through his area, he may find the trailing linebackers running right over him!

There are a total of seven officials on the field. The *referee* stands somewhere behind the offensive backfield and is in charge of the officiating crew. The *umpire* stands behind the defensive line and calls any infractions in that

area of the field. There is a *head linesman* and a *line judge* who stand at opposite ends of the line of scrimmage and are responsible for tracking the forward progress of the ball, plus keeping track of the downs and yardage needed for a first down. The head linesman and line judge are also the official timekeepers. The *field judge* stands behind the secondary and specifically watches punts, kickoffs, and downfield plays. Finally, the *back judge* and the *side judge* keep an eye on the secondary for any infractions.

Each official must be completely familiar with the players and their assignments. Most NFL officials have served for decades at the high school or college level before entering the ranks of the pros. After officiating in college, they must have professional experience with either the Canadian or European league before the NFL will consider them.

According to Steve Wilson, "The league asks us to concentrate seven to ten seconds at a time, looking for anything that is outside the scope of common play. Our goal is to allow the players to play their game while being able to totally describe everything we see in the area of our responsibility at any given time." In the truest sense of the word, Steve and his fellow officials are witnesses.

One of Wilson's favorite stories deals with a young middle linebacker who was extremely talented and very aggressive: "The teams had been very verbal with one another during the contest," he recalls. "The quarterback called a screen, and the middle linebacker read it all the way. He slipped past the blockers and sought out the back that had his gaze fixed on the ball that was slowly drifting his way. With all the power the linebacker could muster, he hit the running back just as the ball arrived." Still recalling the event, Steve described the crash of the two gladiators:

They hit so hard that the running back's helmet flew off and rolled for several yards. The middle linebacker jumped up and started yelling profanities at the disabled player lying on the ground in a daze. It was clear that he was trying to totally intimidate the hurt man and his teammates.

About the time they went to commercial break for the injury timeout, I asked the middle linebacker to clean up his language. I pointed to my lapel mike and reminded him that everything he had said went out over the broadcast and was potentially influencing the audience, including kids and maybe even his family. I reminded him that he was an example, a witness, to others. With a sheepish look, he grabbed my lapel, held the microphone close to his mouth, and shouted, "Mama, I'm sorry; I'm sorry, Mama!" [13]

Francis of Assisi once said, "Preach the gospel at all times and, when necessary, use words." The Christian life is about imitating the character of God in every action and attitude. If we are that kind of witness, we will surely impact people with a love, grace, and mercy that transcend the common boundaries of understanding.

GAME PLAN:

1. Are you an effective witness for Jesus Christ?

2. Do you have fellow believers who are praying for you and your effectiveness as a witness to your family, friends, and coworkers? Read Ephesians 6:19 — ask that they pray this verse for you!

THE WEST COAST OFFENSE HAS BECOME EXTREMELY POPULAR WITH MANY OFFENSIVE COORDINATORS. Operated correctly, it is very difficult to stop. The fast-hitting passing attack and a slash-and-slam running game create a lot of movement and surprise potential.

Some say the original West Coast Offense was a product of Oakland Raider Al Davis or San Diego Charger Sid Gilman, both of whom were very pass-oriented. Others claim that it was the by-product of "the Genius"— Coach Bill Walsh, who guided the 49ers to several Super Bowl victories.

The West Coast Offense has lots of motion from the backs and receivers; repeated short passes allow gifted runners to break tackles in the open field. There is a great deal of zone blocking, and the running backs operate out of single-back or "I" formations.

The key to this offense is deception. One coach said, "It's all about fooling your opponent and keeping him off balance." The quick-hitting offense helps reduce the effectiveness of mobile and agile linebackers who like to blitz. By the time they get to the quarterback, he has already released the ball. In a West Coast Offense, instead of doing a 5- or 7-step drop, the wary quarterback moves 3 steps back and immediately hits a receiver.

Most coaches will agree that three things are needed to make this offense work:

1. Players must be smart and listen carefully to each play call. The average West Coast Offense may have more than 150 plays that involve various men in motion off a basic formation. The players must keep track of where their opponents are, remember the snap count, and be able to move into a new position at the proper time.

2. A team must be patient and disciplined enough to allow the time necessary for all the motion men to do their thing while not false-starting or having two men move simultaneously. It requires that the coach communicate the new play to the quarterback quickly so that he has enough time after breaking the huddle to set his teammates in motion.

3. Receivers must be fast and precise in their patterns—it's all about timing. With an accurate quarterback and a receiver who runs perfect routes, a quick slant is almost unstoppable. If a team needs 5 yards, a quarterback can make a bullet-like throw, low and away from the defender, allowing only his receiver to have a good shot at catching it.

Many of today's NFL coaches who studied under Walsh have taken their initial concepts of his system and have modified their play selection to take advantage of the individual skills and abilities of selected key players. An explosive running attack complements the short passing game. The big and powerful back that lumbers through the line is not as effective as a quicker moving back who can also be used as a receiver.

Too much time in the pocket allows the onrushing defensive players an opportunity to sack the quarterback. In an era when so many starting quarterbacks have been seriously injured, thereby placing the effectiveness of the offense in jeopardy, it is almost a necessity that coaches develop schemes to allow the ball to be delivered to another player within seconds.

To make the West Coast Offense work, you need a wily and seasoned veteran who can see a great deal of the field of play, who carefully selects the most open receiver, who is alert and accurate in his throws. Today there is less of a requirement for the gunner who can whip the ball 70 yards down the field—he is of less value than a ball-controlling, quick-thinking, accurate passer who is able to respond to more situations.

Some time ago I remember reading a book titled *Spirit-Controlled Temperament*, which has long disappeared from my library shelves (along with scores of others loaned out and never returned). What I remember of the book deals with how we need to work at being under control. Our natural, worldly flesh suggests, "If it feels good, do it." However, once we receive Christ into our lives, we are filled with a Spirit that is not of this earth. To some this will sound mystical, yet God intended it to be very understandable: "I will pour out my Spirit on all people" (Joel 2:28, Acts 2:17). The apostle Peter at Pentecost reminded his listeners that they would receive "the gift of the Holy Spirit" if they repented and were baptized (Acts 2:37–39).

I know I need help calling the plays in my life. I appreciate knowing that the ultimate Coach and Counselor runs my West Coast Offense. He can run yours too—just ask God to come into your heart and take over your life. He will help guide you in all your decisions.

GAME PLAN:

1. Is God calling the plays in your life, or are you still trying your own "run and gun" approach?

2. What tactics are you going to institute in your daily walk that will allow you to give God more "play-calling" ability in your life?

« FEATURING »

Mike Waufle

FAVORITE BIBLE VERSE: COLOSSIANS 3:23

Whatever you do, work at it with all your heart,
as working for the Lord, not for men.

As a young person going through the school of hard knocks, I quickly learned that in life it is important to be tenacious in your spirit and determined in your outlook. That is what drives me as a defensive line coach in the NFL and as a Christian man. Some people say I'm relentless, driven, and aggressive, but that's what makes me who I am.

Maybe it was the years I spent in the Marine Corps or working with great coaches like Jeff Fisher, Steve Spagnuolo, Tom Coughlin, and Jon Gruden that shaped my attitudes, but I believe it was many of the leaders found in Scripture. I'm inspired every day by the lives of people like Abraham, King David, Daniel, Ezekiel, Peter, Paul, and of course Jesus—they all had to overcome obstacles in their lives to become winners.

It was an honor to hear recently that an ESPN.com panel of bloggers suggested that I was the top pick as an assistant coach in the league. Whatever talent God has given me has been more than equaled by the numerous talented athletes I've been privileged to coach. It is a truism that offense gets you to the playoffs, but it's defense that brings home the championships. I've had the privilege to coach men like Michael Strahan, Justin Tuck, Osi Umenyiora, Fred Robbins, Jay Alford, Dave Tollefson, and Barry Cofield all who made up the Super Bowl XLII winning defensive line that so dominated Tom Brady and threw him off his game. That year our defensive line led the league with 53 quarterback sacks. Their performance that year turned out to be a high point in keeping with the tradition of building the Giants' teams on rushing the passer.

The 2012, 2008, 1992, and 1987 Super Bowls won by the Giants seem to have the strength of the "crazed dog" defense and their fans in the 1950s who were credited with inventing the now-ubiquitous "DE-FENSE" chant.

As Christians, our defense is connected to our focus on God's game plan for life—the Bible. Don't be led astray by other philosophies or doctrines. Stay with the game-winning Words from our heavenly Father.

> *You are a shield around me, O LORD;*
> *you bestow glory on me and lift up my head.*
> —PSALM 3:3

23 THE INVISIBLE TEAM MEMBER

AVID FOOTBALL FANS OFTEN SAY THAT THE "GREATEST GAME EVER PLAYED" OCCURRED ON A COLD DECEMBER AFTERNOON IN 1958. The powerful New York Giants clashed with the Baltimore Colts and a young quarterback named Johnny Unitas during the first ever NFL overtime game.

On that historic day in 1958, before a roaring crowd of 64,185 in Yankee Stadium, Unitas directed the Colts to a thrilling, come-from-behind, 23–17 overtime victory. The ebb and flow of the game kept fans on the edge of their seats the entire time. The finicky, invisible player "momentum" seemed to vacillate back and forth, unable to choose a winner between the two teams.

Most coaches will tell you that embracing momentum can mean the difference between victory and defeat. There are many things that build momentum during a game. It could be as simple as the ball bouncing your way, or a spectacular achievement by a marquee player, or a previously unknown player who steps up and plays the game of his life. When these things happen, play after play, the team begins to feel confident. They tend to play with more enthusiasm and abandonment. Endorphins pump through their systems, creating a natural increase in energy.

In a similar manner, the Holy Spirit empowers the Christian. Through the Spirit, God gives believers all the spiritual power they need to live a victorious Christian life. When the Spirit enters the life of a new believer, he or she receives new power, enduring strength, and godly wisdom, so that he or she might serve others and grow in the knowledge of God. In Ephesians 3:20, Paul encouraged the new believers in Ephesus to trust that God's Spirit could do far more in their lives than they could ever imagine.

GOD WILL NOT ASK ME
HOW MANY PRO BOWLS
I WAS IN, HE WILL ASK
ME IF I KNEW JESUS.

REGGIE WHITE

Through actual experience, Paul knew of the spiritual resources and power supply that only the Holy Spirit could provide. He was regularly challenged—physically, emotionally, and spiritually—yet he found peace and comfort in the energy of the Comforter: "We are afflicted in every way, but not crushed; perplexed, but not despairing; persecuted, but not forsaken; struck down, but not destroyed" (2 Corinthians 4:8–9 NASB).

As with momentum in a game, we can win at life if we utilize the power of the Spirit. When you encounter fear, frustrations, failures, threats, or sickness, remember the Holy Spirit is your true source of strength and might. And unlike the invisible player (momentum), who is sometimes fickle, you can count on God's comfort to remain true to the end.

> *[He] is able to do far more abundantly beyond all that we ask or think, according to the power that works within us.*
>
> —EPHESIANS 3:20 NASB

GAME PLAN:

1. Make it a point, on a daily basis, to ask God to bless you with the endurance and wisdom needed to serve in a manner that brings glory and honor to Him.

IN 1984, DAN MARINO SET LEAGUE RECORDS BY COMPLETING 48 TOUCHDOWN PASSES AND GAINING 5,084 PASSING YARDS FOR THE MIAMI DOLPHINS. His touchdown pass record stood for 20 years until it was broken in 2004 by Peyton Manning and then again by Tom Brady. In 2011, Drew Brees finally broke Marino's passing record with 5,087 yards. Great quarterbacks all!

As I study first-rate quarterbacks and survey literature on their position, it seems that Tom Bass was correct in his analysis of the "playmakers." In his book, *Play Football the NFL Way*, he tells us there are four critical elements to being a successful passer:

1. The *set* is the quarterback's drop-back. A good plant on his back foot is critical in transferring his momentum into his throwing arm.
2. The *forward step* shifts the quarterback's direction and directs his energy toward his receiver.
3. The *release* or *delivery* is the most critical stage. The "hips of the player should open up and be square with the target area." The quarterback should throw the ball with "the trunk of his body and not merely his arm."
4. The body's *follow-through* after releasing the ball is fundamental to the pass's final outcome.

The steps needed for having a solid relationship with God are much like

NO WONDER CENTERS GET CONFUSED.
THEY'RE ALWAYS LOOKING AT THE WORLD
UPSIDE DOWN AND BACKWARDS.

BOB ZUPPKE,
Former Illinois Coach

the elements for being a successful passer. We must *set* our minds and hearts in a new direction by first stopping the backward slide of negative character flaws that bring us to sin. The *forward step* is important as we begin to move toward God's plan for our life. As we open up and become square with Him, our spirit is *released* for service; He sees our heart and forgives us for our past failures. Finally, we must commit to the *follow-through*—if we are sincere, there should be a change of heart, a change of attitude, and a change of actions, reflecting God's Spirit and love within us.

Let's make sure our grip on life is firm. And most importantly, let's keep on working toward perfecting those character traits that glorify God.

> *Now change your mind and attitude to God*
> *and turn to him so he can cleanse away your*
> *sins and send you wonderful times of*
> *refreshment from the presence of the Lord.*
> —ACTS 3:19 TLB

GAME PLAN:

1. Which one of the four elements outlined above do you struggle with most in your relationship with God?

2. What tactics can you employ to improve your ability to execute that element and deepen your ability to glorify God through your relationship with Him?

25 CHARACTER IS EVERYTHING

I TRY TO WATCH AT LEAST THIRTY MINUTES OF ESPN EACH DAY IN ORDER TO CATCH UP ON ALL THE HAPPENINGS. Several years back, I observed a conversation between Keyshawn Johnson and an ESPN reporter. Keyshawn had just signed a multiyear contract that made him the highest-paid wide receiver in the NFL at that time. It was noteworthy that the reporter seemed more interested in talking to Keyshawn about the importance of athletes becoming good role models than concentrating so much on the monetary rewards associated with being a superstar.

In *The Message*, Eugene Peterson's paraphrase of the New Testament, he elaborated on the apostle Paul's words to Timothy:

> *Concentrate on doing your best for God, work you won't be ashamed of, laying out the truth plain and simple. Stay clear of pious talk that is only talk. Words are not mere words, you know. If they're not backed by a godly life, they accumulate as poison in the soul. (2 Timothy 2:15–17)*

It's about integrity, my friend. As the nineteenth-century writer Charles Reade once said, "Sow a thought, and you reap an act; sow an act, and you reap a habit; sow a habit, and you reap a character; sow a character, and you reap a destiny."

Chuck Swindoll reminds us, "And so it remains, our character is more important than our position; more important than our fame; more important than any glory; more important than our power, and more vital to our country and families than ever before." [14]

FOOTBALL IS LIKE
LIFE, IT REQUIRES
PERSEVERANCE,
SELF-DENIAL, HARD
WORK, SACRIFICE,
DEDICATION, AND
RESPECT FOR
AUTHORITY.

VINCE LOMBARDI

Character and integrity are interchangeable; they mean "doing right on purpose." As the psalmist put it, "Let the LORD judge the peoples. Judge me, O LORD, according to my righteousness, according to my integrity, O Most High" (Psalm 7:8).

The man of integrity walks securely.
—PROVERBS 10:9

GAME PLAN:

1. 2 Corinthians 1:12 says, "Now this is our boast: Our conscience testifies that we have conducted ourselves in the world, and especially in our relations with you, in the holiness and sincerity that are from God. We have done so not according to worldly wisdom but according to God's grace." Take a moment to reflect on your interactions with family, friends, coworkers, and the people you encounter on a daily basis. Can the same be said of you?

2. Does your character speak well for you and does it exemplify Christ-like attributes?

THE HEAD COACH

IN 1996, THE CHAPLAIN OF THE CALIFORNIA BEARS COLLEGE FOOTBALL TEAM AND ITS THEN HEAD COACH, Steve Mariucci, invited me to present a message to the team before their Saturday game. As is my custom, I arrived early to check out the surroundings and to have some quiet time before being introduced.

Much to my surprise, the first group to appear was Coach Mariucci and several of his assistant coaches. After introducing himself, he told me that chapel was an important part of his team's pregame preparation, and he encouraged all his players to attend.

Shortly after my message, Mariucci and I discussed the importance of spending regular time reading God's Word and being encouraged by others. Before leaving for the game, I promised to provide him with some type of inspirational message on a weekly basis. In order to properly prepare these spiritual vignettes, I endeavored to become acquainted with the type of pressures and concerns facing men in his position.

At the end of that exciting season, Mariucci was invited to be the head coach for the San Francisco 49ers. The pressure of being one of the league's youngest head coaches, coupled with the chaos in the front office, proved to be a real challenge even for this gifted man. However, even with all that pressure, Mariucci's faith, abilities, talent, and patience provided the ingredients needed to be very effective and to survive.

What is it that empowers a man to endure the trials of being a head coach? How can a person survive the onslaught of the combined pressure from prima donna players, front-office demands, community scrutiny, and family needs? The great collegiate coach Lou Holtz once said this about the uncertainties of his profession: "One day you're drinking wine, and the next day you're picking the grapes."

President Harry Truman had a solid insight on the unique pressures of coaching: "It's a lot tougher to be a football coach than a president. You've got four years as a president, and they guard you. A coach doesn't have anyone to protect him when things go wrong."

The enduring owners and fans of the past have been replaced with demands for instant success from coaches who have yet to gain the wisdom and experience that only trials and tribulation can bring. Would the media and fans of today be patient and visionary during the tough times that it took to shape the great coaches of the past?

We hold in high esteem coaches who are able to effectively manage chaos and confusion. They must be multitalented in all aspects of the game and be able to select and manage outstanding position coaches who can effectively communicate and motivate their players to get the job done. Coaches like these are difficult to find and even harder to keep. They possess unique capabilities to remain in control and poised even during times of personal attack.

In Gene Getz's wonderful book *The Measure of a Man*, he discusses what it takes to be a man of God. His thoughts about the apostle Paul are fascinating to contemplate. Paul commended those who wish to lead: "It is a fine work he desires to do" (1 Timothy 3:1 NASB). But Paul further explained that any potential leader should make sure that he or she is a certain kind of person. We must be beyond reproach, temperate, self-controlled, respectable, gentle, and able to manage our families. Getz also tells us that these characteristics are shaped and formed during trials and tribulations *over a period of time.* [15] The measure of God's man begins by refining and perfecting our lives (1 Timothy 3:2–7, Titus 1:6–8).

The logical question for someone wishing to become a better person is "Where do I begin?" The answer is to take each of these characteristics, understand what they mean, and set out in a direction to refine your character hour by hour and day by day to incorporate a Chrislike character.

> *He must be hospitable, one who loves what is good,*
> *who is self-controlled, upright, holy and disciplined.*
> —TITUS 1:8

GAME PLAN:

1. From the list above, what are the areas in your own life that you need to refine and perfect?

2. How do you intend to work on those areas? I would encourage you to seek out wise counsel (perhaps your pastor or another godly man from your church), meet with him and ask him to help you create a plan of action that will help you work on those identified areas of concern.

IN THEIR EXCELLENT ARTICLE TITLED "ABSOLUTELY INTENSE," as seen in the November issue of *Sharing the Victory* (published by the Fellowship of Christian Athletes), Allen Palmeri and Joan Bustos wrote about the passion and focus of the Jets' head coach, Herman Edwards.

Contained within this work is some revealing material about what shaped the life of this prestigious NFL coach, now sports commentator. As a young high school and college player, Edwards was a cocky, brash athlete with a big Afro and a bigger ego. His hard-hitting style of play was second only to his quickness and confidence.

As a cornerback, he patterned his speed and attitude after Dallas Cowboys All-Pro wide receiver Bob Hayes. Edwards insisted that coaches liken him to the world-class Olympian and call him "Mr. Bob."

Edwards was drafted by the Philadelphia Eagles and ended his career with 33 interceptions, starting 135 games as an Eagle and reportedly never missing a practice at any level of football. As commendable as his work ethic was, more rewarding was his commitment to becoming a believer.

As Edwards went into coaching with the Kansas City Chiefs, the "Mr. Bob" persona was dropped. The smug personality he had before receiving Christ was put aside for a confident and self-assured spirit that impacted his fellow coaches and players.

In 1996, Edwards left the Chiefs to take a position in Tampa Bay under his longtime mentor and friend Tony Dungy. Dungy implanted great wisdom, supreme confidence, and even more mental toughness into Edwards' life. Accepting a job as head coach on the world's largest stage—as Edwards later did in New York City for the Jets, and then later with the Kansas City

Chiefs—requires a special inner sturdiness. The difference between Edwards and a few other hardworking coaches is that he is willing to stand up and be held accountable for his faith in Jesus Christ.

Herman Edwards actually liked the toughness of standing for Christ in the public arena, and he accepted the reality that there is ridicule awaiting anyone who takes this position as a believer in Jesus. It seems the more a person excels, the more of a target he or she becomes. The reward a high-profile person receives for following the right path is that he or she is presented with amazing opportunities to influence others in a positive direction.

Few things are more encouraging than watching a prominent Christian remain faithful under fire. Whether it's the president of the United States, a great community leader, or the head coach of an NFL team, the effect is the same. Someone has said, "The furnace of individual trials and persecution is designed by God for the purpose of melting away the debris of our personal lives and purifying what is left." Edwards obviously knew that, or he would not have embraced the testing of his faith.

When Edwards shares his life and testimony, he usually quotes Proverbs 22:1: "It's better to have a good name than all the riches in the world" (author's paraphrase). Throughout his coaching career he remained under control and steadfast to the principles found in God's Word.

A good name and a respectable reputation helped Edwards walk the "unseen journey" of faith. Most coaches continually ask their teams to provide maximum effort and intense focus while playing with great passion. They bark at their teams when a player loses control and gets a penalty. Yet many passionate coaches fail to realize the importance of modeling the same principles of self-discipline they try to coach into their players.

Behavior and language that are on the verge of losing control don't model an appropriate attitude. In my experience as a chaplain, I have seen that on a team of 53 players, 20 to 40 percent of the guys attend chapel and *want* to be associated with Christians. While playing to win, those players who are really committed to their faith desire to model Christlike behavior.

When a coach loses his temper, exhibits inappropriate behavior, or uses blasphemous language, it drives a penetrating wound into the soul of a believer. I've talked to players who tell me their attitudes and actions on the field are in part a result of how a coach manages his tongue. It's not about judging or condemning coaches who seem to think that being verbally abusive is a way to motivate players. It's also not about being perfect, for we all have sinned and fall short of God's standard (Romans 3:23). While grace should be the reality that most occupies a believer's spirit, it is important for others to see the wisdom found in the style and management success that marks a man like Herman Edwards.

Edwards is no less effective because he models his faith. A former teammate stated, "Herman is a class act. [But] is he intense and effective? Absolutely!"

GAME PLAN:

1. Do your words and actions reflect your faith? Are there areas you need to work on?

2. What steps are you going to take to make sure that you consistently model Christlike behavior to those around you?

28 THE "O" LINE

WITHOUT MUCH FAME OR RECOGNITION, THE OFFENSIVE LINE DOES ITS JOB. Despite all the media attention that marquee quarterbacks and running backs receive, without a great offensive line the quarterback wouldn't have time to complete many passes and the running back wouldn't have the holes to shoot through. A good offensive line can take many years to build and—with injury or trade or free agency—only minutes to fall apart.

In football, blocking is one of the most important skills and also one of the least appreciated. Former Super Bowl Coach of the Oakland Raiders and former television commentator, John Madden said, "You can design the best offensive plays in football, but if your blockers don't do their job, those plays are worthless." For this reason Madden and many coaches believe that assembling the right group of powerful players to make up the "O" line is perhaps the most important task in football.

If a team is playing well on offense, it's usually because the offensive line is having a good day against the opposing defensive line. Holes open up more quickly for the running backs, and quarterbacks have the necessary time to scope the field and pick out open receivers.

However, it's rare to hear much about the offensive line unless someone misses a block or lets his man sack the quarterback. Unlike the more high-profile defensive linemen who usually have nicknames, offensive linemen are normally the quiet warriors of the game. Statistics indicate that these humble but powerful giants are usually the brightest men on the field; most finished college with good grades. They often take on a leadership role within the team, while becoming mentors to the younger players.

As we study the character of God, we see illustrations of His power all around us—evidence in creation, in changing circumstances, in miracles, and in changed lives. Just as the offensive line protects the quarterback from powerful attacks, God protects people from attacks. First Corinthians 10:13 tells us that "No temptation has overtaken you except such as is common to man; but God *is* faithful" (NKJV).

Relying on God's power gives us confidence, strength, assurance, direction, and boldness to live the Christian life as He intended. Whatever trouble we have on earth, we need to remember that we have an awesome God who is capable of handling our problems. God "is able to do far more abundantly beyond all that we ask or think, according to the power that works within us" (Ephesians 3:20 NASB).

During the tough times God wants us to keep focused on the big picture. Remember, our eternal hope rests on His power, the power that saved us and will "raise [us] up on the last day" (John 6:40 NASB). That should be the great hope of all Christians—especially those who are enduring major struggles. Praise God that our heavenly destiny is secure, infinitely more secure than anything on earth.

Yet those who wait for the LORD will gain new strength; . . . they will run and not get tired, they will walk and not become weary.

—ISAIAH 40:31 NASB

WE SHOULD'VE WON,
BUT UNITAS IS A GUY WHO KNOWS WHAT
IT WAS TO EAT POTATO SOUP SEVEN DAYS
A WEEK AS A KID. THAT'S WHAT BEAT US.

Norm Van Brocklin,
Former Rams Coach, after losing to the Colts

GAME PLAN:

1. When you face tough times, do you rely upon God's power or your own strength? He can direct, equip, and guide you in each decision and action. And like a great lineman, God will quickly open up holes of opportunity for you to glide through on your way to success.

2. Read Ephesians 6:13–19 where Paul discussed putting on the armor of God. Pray that God will help you remember to suit up every day.

HALFTIME IS TO A FOOTBALL GAME WHAT INTERMISSION IS TO FINE OPERA. It's a chance for the participants to catch their breath and reevaluate personal goals. And it's a time for coaches to make timely adjustments in the game plan and modify their offensive and defensive alignments to take better advantage of their opponent's weaknesses.

Unlike what we occasionally see on video clips, there usually isn't much in the way of a "Knute Rockne" speech by most head coaches. Once they exit the field, players grab a sports drink and some energy bars as a quick snack while they sit down and listen to their position coaches.

While the halftime entertainers take their final bow, the head coach usually reminds the players about the importance of the game and encourages everyone to play to his potential. But in 1928, Notre Dame's head coach, Knute Rockne, gave his halftime team a challenge that has yet to be forgotten: "Win one for the Gipper." Rockne's goal was to motivate his players to leave it all on the field. It had its desired effect: Notre Dame won over a very tough Army team 12–6 on a touchdown pass from Butch Niemiec to Johnny O'Brien in the closing minutes of the game.

A few years before, George Gipp was a quiet and unassuming triple threat (runner, passer, and kicker) for Notre Dame. He had great confidence and inspired others with his dedicated efforts. Rockne later recalled, "I learned very early to place full confidence in his self-confidence." Had there been a Heisman Trophy that year, most coaches felt George Gipp would have received it.

In 1920, Notre Dame finished its season with a 25–0 victory over Michigan State, but their dedicated Gipp was in the college infirmary at

South Bend with a life-threatening infection. Antibiotic drugs had not yet been developed, and Gipp's condition was worsening by the day. In the last few hours before his passing, Coach Rockne made one of his daily visits to see Gipp. The lanky collegiate All-Star looked into his coach's eyes and said, "Some time, Rock, when the team is up against it, when things are wrong and the breaks are beating the boys, ask them to go in there with all they've got and win just one for the Gipper. I don't know where I'll be then, Rock. But I'll know about it, and I'll be happy."

For eight years Rockne thought about the proper time to encourage his players with the deathbed words of this dedicated athlete. Many on the 1928 Notre Dame team knew of George Gipp and had actually been in the same grammar school with the legendary running back. The motivation and inspiration of Rockne's famous locker-room words helped guide Notre Dame to a victory and won the hearts of millions of future fans.

We all need to take an occasional halftime break—to be inspired and to restore our spiritual passion. All of us need an opportunity to reassess our lives and to refocus priorities. We live in a hurried culture with instant every-thing. Stress abounds in the workplace as well as in many homes. Our attention can easily become riveted on the temporal and the material as we desperately seek to provide a "better way of life" for our families. But this is not unique to our time. Even the disciples needed an occasional halftime break. According to the gospel of Mark, the disciples had gone out in pairs and had been teaching, preaching, and healing throughout the countryside. After laboring day and night, they received some devastating information. Their friend John the Baptist had been beheaded. The exhausted and emo-tionally troubled group now needed the comfort and companionship of their Lord.

They returned to the Galilee area and found Jesus. My Bible is open to Mark 6:31–32, where we pick up the story: "Then, because so many people were coming and going that they did not even have a chance to eat, [Jesus] said to them, 'Come with me by yourselves to a quiet place and get some rest.' So they went away by themselves in a boat to a solitary place."

Scripture encourages us to take regular "halftime breaks" to be alone with God. We are to catch our spiritual breath by focusing upon His goodness, mercy, love, power, encouragement, grace, and kindness. God's Word commands us to periodically surrender the hectic pace of everyday life and find that quiet spot where the distractions and tensions of our environment can be screened out. I think I just heard the halftime whistle blow. How about you?

Be still, and know that I am God.
—PSALM 46:10

GAME PLAN:

1. When is your next halftime?

2. How can you be more intentional in building times of rest and rejuvenation into your busy schedule?

IT HAS BEEN CALLED THE "GREATEST SIN-GLE-SEASON SPORTS STORY IN HISTORY!" [16] Kurt Warner's long road to gridiron success was filled with setbacks and bad breaks. He warmed the bench for four years at the University of Northern Iowa. Finally getting a chance as a fifth-year senior, he led the Panthers to the NCAA Division 1-AA semifinals and was named the Gateway Conference Offensive Player of the Year. But he was passed over in the NFL draft and rejected by the Canadian Football League. When all else failed, Warner took a job stocking shelves for $5.50 an hour at the Hy-Vee Supermarket in Cedar Falls, Iowa, while he worked out at a college practice field during his time off.

A year later he was playing again, but in small-time Arena League football, an indoor game using eight players on a side and 50-yard fields. He missed a tryout for the Chicago Bears in 1997 when he was bitten on the elbow by a venomous spider, leaving him unable to throw.

After three years he took a step up. In 1998, he was signed by the Rams and was sent to the Amsterdam Admirals of NFL Europe, where in the spring of that year he led the league in passing yardage and touchdowns.

The Rams put him on the team for the 1998–1999 season, but he played in only one game. He was left unprotected in the expansion draft, but the new Cleveland Browns didn't want him. Warner was still with the Rams in early 1999 at minimum pay, but they didn't appreciate his full potential and signed quarterback Trent Green before the season for $16.5 million. It looked like Warner would be riding the bench again as a backup.

But Green got hurt, and it opened the door for Warner to show his stuff. By the end of the playoffs, much to the surprise of almost everyone, he had thrown a record 49 touchdown passes, led the league in completion percentage, and taken the Rams to the best record in the NFC: 13–3. His 109.2 quarterback rating put him in the same class as his idols, Joe Montana and Steve Young. In five months he had gone from anonymity to being a Pro Bowler and an NFL MVP. He capped off a Cinderella season by passing the Rams to victory in Super Bowl XXXIV. He not only won the game, but also the hearts of many Americans.

Through it all Warner remembered his faith, his family, and his friends. He believes it is important to keep "first things first." His great humility was underscored when he stood before a Billy Graham Crusade audience of more than forty thousand and said, "Whether I'm a Super Bowl Champion or a regular guy stocking groceries at the Hy-Vee, sharing my faith and glorifying Jesus is the central focus of my time on this earth. . . . I want to be a role model for Christ in everything I do."

In a time when so many players are looking for every opportunity to beat their own drum, it is refreshing to see a man as humble as Kurt Warner. He and his lovely wife, Brenda, continually work with their seven kids on developing great character.

I'm reminded of numerous verses in Scripture that help me appreciate that whatever our gifts and talents are, whatever we're able to do from a physical, mental, or spiritual standpoint, or whatever our perceived successes, *we owe it all to God*. Moses told the Israelites before they entered the Promised Land: "You may say in your heart, 'My power and the strength of my hand made me this wealth.' But you shall remember the LORD your God, for it is He who is giving you power to make wealth" (Deuteronomy 8:17–18 NASB).

The Warners realize that everything they have, everything they are, is because of God's grace and strength in their lives. Satan will tempt us to be prideful and haughty in spirit because of our abilities and accomplishments, but we must realize that every good thing we have is from the Lord. Paul asked us, "What do you have that you did not receive?" (1 Corinthians 4:7 NASB).

I believe God wants us to have a "healthy pride" in what we do, but not be prideful. He wants us to do our very best in everything—try to work hard in our jobs, develop relationships, and encourage our families in serving Him. He has shown us by example that it is good to be joyful after we have accomplished something wonderful. In Genesis 1, we see God affirming Himself after each creation by saying, "It is good." And when He finished creating man and woman He said, "It is *very* good" (emphasis added).

Pride, like many other things, is a two-edged sword. It can be used to glorify God, or it can be used to disgrace and embarrass our heavenly Father, friends, and family. Kurt Warner and many other Christian athletes realize who has empowered them and who ultimately should receive the credit.

GAME PLAN:

1. What are some ways that pride of self creeps up in your own life?

2. What are some effective ways to battle selfish pride?

« FEATURING »

Steve Spagnuolo

FAVORITE BIBLE VERSE: HEBREWS 11:1

*Now faith is being sure of what we hope for
and certain of what we do not see.*

In the NFL coaching world, we often blurt out comments like, "There are only two kinds of coaches in this business: those who have been fired and those who will be." It is hard to believe, but since the days of the AFL there have been over 400 head coaches. Only a few have escaped the unfortunate experience of being "let go." Even some of the great legends—like Tom Landry, who coached 29 consecutive seasons for the Dallas Cowboys from 1960–1988; Curly Lambeau, who coached 29 consecutive years for the Green Bay Packers from 1921–1949; Don Shula, who coached 26 consecutive years for the Miami Dolphins from 1970–1995; Chuck Noll, who coached for 23 consecutive seasons with the Pittsburgh Steelers; and the great George Halas, who coached for 40 total seasons for the Chicago Bears— were dismissed by their teams.

Today, Andy Reid stands alone with a 13-year run with the Philadelphia Eagles, never having been fired as a head coach. Even Bill Belichick, who went on to become a Hall of Fame head coach, faced the unfortunate fate after a 5-year run in Cleveland. Now Andy is on top of the pile as a tenure coach with the Eagles. After only three seasons in St. Louis, my dismissal as head coach of the Rams came as no surprise, but it still impacted my family and me greatly.

I loved the people I worked with, especially the coaches and players. I very much appreciated their hard work and dedication. Each loss we faced was heartfelt and created a drive within me and my staff to try and develop the components necessary to become a successful team. Much like Tony Dungy's departing with the Buccaneers, my time ran out.

I've seen too many coaches put their faith in an owner or in a team only to be emotionally devastated when their "pink slip" arrived. I have learned that if you are going to survive the "wild ride" as an NFL coach, you better have a supportive wife, understanding family, loyal friends, a courageous heart, and a great faith in God.

I've come to appreciate that faith doesn't depend on me having my way; faith depends on God having His way. During trying times of illness or death, when facing uncertainty about the future, or when separation, loss, and grief bring on unavoidable stress or temptation, it is your faith in the Almighty and the love of His Son that brings you through the trials.

I am blessed to have a special wife, Maria, who is not only loving and supportive but also is a constant example of how to live a faithful Christian life. She often encourages me with her words just as James did with the words he gave us: "My brethren, count it all joy when you fall into various trials, knowing that the testing of your faith produces patience. . . . Blessed is the man who endures temptation; for when he has been approved, he will receive the crown of life which the Lord has promised to those who love Him" (James 1:2–3, 12 NKJV).

I do not know what the future holds, but whatever my lot in life, I will remain faithful to my God and family. I will define my character and dedication not by what position I hold but by the relationship I have with my Lord and heavenly Father.

SOME CONSIDER OFFENSIVE LINEMEN TO BE BIG, STRONG BODIES WHO ARE NOT SMART ENOUGH OR SKILLED ENOUGH TO PLAY A "RESPECTABLE POSITION." In 1968, when Paul Brown took command of the expansion Cincinnati Bengals, the first player he drafted wasn't a quarterback or a running back or a defensive lineman. He selected Bob Johnson, a center from the University of Tennessee.

"With this young man," Brown said, "we have a player who will anchor our offensive line for the next decade." Johnson went on to play twelve seasons, helping the Bengals develop into a consistent contender.

I believe the inspiration for Brown's decision came from observing former University of Miami center Jim Otto. At 205 pounds, many considered Jim too small to play professional football. However, his exceptional desire, positive spirit, and keen insights into the game of football quickly propelled this unlikely player into becoming one of the NFL's greatest stars.

Upon entering the newly developed American Football Conference in 1960, Otto's dedicated work ethic inspired his fellow players. His consistency and durability is now legendary—he started every regular season game for the next fifteen years. For thirteen straight seasons, he was All-Pro, the only All-AFC center in the league's history.

As number "00" developed into a superstar, so did his team. The Oakland Raiders' win-loss record while Jim snapped the ball was impressive: seven divisional championships in an eight-year period, plus a Super Bowl win. Jim was inducted into the Pro Football Hall of Fame on August 2, 1980. He was so well respected that he was accepted in his first year of eligibility, only the third

AFC graduate to be so honored. "He loved to win. He led by example, and he set the tempo," his longtime teammate George Blanda said. "He gave the Raiders an image of hard discipline, hard work, and hard-nosed football."

To be a great center like Otto, you need to be a sure-handed ball-snapper and a superior blocker who seeks out targets far beyond the limited area immediately in front of your position. The center also has the burden of calling blocking signals for the offensive line. If he makes mental errors, the quarterback or running back has a face-to-face encounter with the defense. A first-rate center needs to have wisdom, quickness, agility, discipline, and stamina.

Because of Otto's dedication, he has been called the "Iron Man of Football." Having now endured thirty-eight repair operations, the descriptions of which could fill a medical encyclopedia, he continues to persevere. He is currently the Special Projects Coordinator and general ombudsman for the Oakland Raiders, and a great spokesman for the NFL and his Lord Jesus Christ. It's no wonder that many coaches consider the center, aside from the quarterback, as having the most important offensive position on the field. Most other linemen can concentrate solely on their assigned blocking tasks, but the center must focus on recognizing the defensive alignment, calling the appropriate blocking assignments, remembering the snap count, snapping the ball, then preparing himself both mentally and physically to take a beating from onrushing linemen and linebackers. "Knowing he's going to get blasted as soon as he snaps the ball, a center needs more mental discipline than anybody at any other position," said former commentator John Madden.

Because every play except kickoff begins with the center's snap and ends with the center determining where the next huddle will be established, there is probably not a more critical player to the functioning of the offense. Many describe the center as the anchor or foundation of the team.

So it is with a true disciple of Christ. He lines up daily to "take the shots" the world hands out, knowing that on any given day he may have to face hatred, bitterness, jealousy, pride, dishonesty, greed, sexual temptation, trickery, and deceit. Paul testified, "Our struggle is not against flesh and blood, but against the rulers, against the authorities, against the powers of this dark world and against the spiritual forces of evil in the heavenly realms" (Ephesians 6:12).

If we are to be the anchor of faithfulness and holiness at work, at home, and in our communities, we must properly prepare ourselves so that we might play to win the game of life. Like the center, we must be tough, determined, committed, and dedicated to the effort. We must mentally prepare ourselves through prayer, and then we must (figuratively speaking) don our protective equipment: "Put on the full armor of God so that you can take your stand against the devil's schemes" (Ephesians 6:11).

Finally, we must spiritually commit ourselves to the game. Several NFL coaches I have talked with tell me they like to have committed Christians on their team because they are good role models, dependable workers, have a good work ethic, stay out of trouble, and know the meaning of sacrifice.

Let's make sure our Christian walk makes us someone that others would want to have on their team.

GAME PLAN:

1. How can you better anchor yourself to Christ so that you're a more effective parent, grandparent, friend, spouse, and coworker?

2. What aspects of your life need to be more fully committed to Christ? Choose to give Him full authority and Lordship over those areas now.

ONE OF THE MAIN ATTRIBUTES OF A SUCCESSFUL QUARTERBACK IS ENORMOUS PATIENCE. It takes patience (and trust) to wait in the pocket until one of your receivers finally breaks open. It takes patience to know that in the 2-minute drill at the end of a close game there is still plenty of time to move up the field and score. Patience is needed in attacking a defense after your team has received a 10-yard penalty for holding. A patient quarterback will not try to move the ball 20 yards in one play if the pass seems too risky. He will use two or three plays that have a higher probability of success in obtaining the necessary yardage.

In a similar manner patience is also required for a running back to wait upon his linemen to complete their blocks so that a hole can be opened up. A linebacker often must be patient as the play develops before he commits himself to an appropriate response. A kicker is all about patience as he waits for the long snapper and holder to properly get the ball into the perfect position before he begins his move to the ball.

Patience is truly a great virtue in professional football. Waiting for the right opportunity to take advantage of a break might mean the difference between success and failure. Outside of a person's family and faith, few things can take the place of patience. Talent will not do it—nothing is more common than unsuccessful men with talent. Genius will not do it—unrewarded brilliance is almost a proverb. Patience and determination are of supreme importance.

In our instant, microwave, drive-through, I-want-it-now culture, patience is hard to come by. We get impatient waiting five seconds for our computer screen to organize itself. We change lines at the supermarket if we see more than three people ahead of us. We are a driven society, and with that we get more and more opportunities for misunderstandings, inappropriate conclusions, and losses of temper.

God's Word tells us that mature believers are marked by patience. In the Greek, *patience* is defined as being "long-tempered" or "long-suffering." In Scripture, we see at least three aspects of biblical patience that should encourage every reader.

First, patience never gives in to negative circumstances, no matter how difficult. God told Abraham He would make him into a great nation and give the promised land to his descendants (Genesis 12:2, 7). When God made this promise, Abraham and Sarah had no children. They had to wait far beyond their childbearing years before God gave them a son. But Hebrews 6:15 says, "Having patiently waited, [Abraham] obtained the promise" (NASB).

A second part of patience is coping with difficult people. Professional football is not much different from public administration, business, or ministry. Personalities don't always mix, management styles differ, expectations vary, and misunderstandings occur. The nature of the pressures and stressors in life can produce friction. Paul told us to "be patient with everyone" (1 Thessalonians 5:14), especially those of the "household of the faith" (Galatians 6:10). This is gentleness, grace, and mercy, especially for those who share our belief in Jesus.

Finally, patience accepts God's plan for everything. A patient person says, "We know that God causes all things to work together for good to those who love God, to those who are called according to His purpose" (Romans 8:28 NASB). This is a reminder to all of us that since God is in control, we can be patient, waiting for Him to work out His will. If we are having problems with wanting to control things, maybe we need to give it all to Jesus!

HE'S SO SHORT HIS BREATH SMELLS OF EARTHWORMS.

RON MEYER,
Former SMU Coach,
on 5'9" guard Harvey McAtee

Therefore, as God's chosen people,
holy and dearly loved, clothe yourselves
with compassion, kindness, humility,
gentleness and patience.
—COLOSSIANS 3:12

GAME PLAN:

1. Where is your focus today? Is it on your problems or on the words of truth found throughout Scripture?

2. Are you struggling with a fellow brother or sister in the Lord? If so, start praying for patience in your dealings with him or her.

3. In difficult situations, are you willing to call upon the Lord, be patient, and let Him work through the issue?

HOW OFTEN HAVE YOU HEARD A COMMENTATOR OR A COACH TALK ABOUT A PLAYER MISSING A CATCH OR HANDOFF BECAUSE HE TOOK HIS EYES OFF THE BALL? A good receiver "looks the ball" into his hand—his gaze is so fixed on the spiraling leather that a defender hitting him seems like a distant possibility. With a similar focus, the running back charges to the line of scrimmage, relying upon the quarterback's eyes and timing to carefully spot the ball into the pocket created with the runner's arms.

It is critical to the ultimate success of a football player to have excellent hand–eye coordination. Even defensive linemen have their special eyes-on-the-ball drill in order to help them become better focused. Mike Waufle, defensive line coach for the St. Louis Rams utilized a painted green football connected to a long string as an aid to help his linemen focus on the ball's movement. As he snatched the grass-colored ball from the turf, the linemen had to carefully time their charge with any motion in it. "I like to see my linemen so focused on ball movement that they rivet their attention on the very tip of the ball," he said. "Usually a player will pick up that the ball is being snapped when the tip of the ball begins to move." [17]

The split-second difference in a lineman picking up the snap can make the difference in delivering the attack or waiting for it to come to him. A lineman's catlike quickness can be a positive factor only when he fixes his gaze on the ball.

During the three-plus years Jesus spent with His disciples, they witnessed many miracles. The apostle Peter was particularly impressed as he watched his Savior walk toward him on water. His immediate response was,

"Lord, if it's you . . . tell me to come to you" (Matthew 14:28). Peter was a lot like many of us—impulsively direct! He wanted to step out in faith and be with Jesus.

Jesus said, "Come." Peter *fixed his gaze upon the Lord* and stepped onto the water. He did not walk around the boat or head off to a better fishing hole; he walked straight toward Jesus. What happened to Peter next is the same thing that happens to all of us when we take our focus off the Master—we sink, or in football vernacular, we fumble the handoff or drop the pass or mistime the snap: "But when [Peter] saw the wind, he was afraid and, beginning to sink, cried out, 'Lord, save me!'" (Matthew 14:30).

Peter broke contact with Jesus the moment his gaze became fixated on the wind and the waves. Just like a receiver who becomes distracted by a defensive back closing in on him, his concentration was broken. Once we place our attention outside the object of our focus, we risk missing an opportunity to be successful.

When we are truly centered upon the Lord with our prayer life, our worship, and our actions, He will handle our problems and help conquer our fears. The Holy Spirit makes us strong and able to walk boldly and with confidence (Proverbs 3:26). As we keep focused on Jesus, all else in our lives will be seen in proper perspective with less chance of a major fumble. No problem is too big—for He is always with us.

Let us fix our eyes on Jesus,
the author and perfecter of our faith.
—HEBREWS 12:2

**WHEN HE GOES INTO A RESTAURANT,
HE DOESN'T ASK FOR A MENU,
HE ASKS FOR AN ESTIMATE.**

TONY KORNHEISER,
Sportswriter, on William "The Refrigerator" Perry

GAME PLAN:

1. What distracts you from keeping your focus on Christ?

2. What needs to be done to reduce or possibly eliminate those distractions?

3. Pray to God that He will help you identify the distractions in your life that need to be dealt with so that you can keep your eyes upon Him.

I REALLY ENJOY WATCHING A GOOD GAME OF FOOTBALL. There's something about the strategy and the teamwork that generates a great deal of excitement. I particularly enjoy watching the decision makers—the coaches. They are filled with so much energy while being driven by their passions to excel. They don't sit back and wait for things to happen. A good coach fully participates in the process of assisting others to do their very best.

Despite disappointment, they persevere! A great coach must have the ability to set aside temporary criticism so that he can focus upon the ultimate goal of the team. Even in defeat these visionaries see opportunities to help build character in themselves and their players. Anyone can be positive and display good character when a team is winning. But it takes a man of real faith and confidence to stay focused and committed when trials prevail. Being a participant requires strength of character.

I really miss the relaxed, easygoing personality of retired New Orleans Saints coach Bum Phillips. He had a way of putting things into perspective. During the very difficult 1985 season, the Saints had lost several close games, as well as three members of the offensive line. They were scheduled to play the San Francisco 49ers, and Bum's job was on the line. When a reporter asked him, "Do you feel any added pressure to win this season?" Bum responded, "No more pressure than before. All they can do is fire me. They can't kill me or eat me." [18]

Most training camps start off with 80 to 85 men. By the time they reach their first regular season game, they will have to trim their rosters to 53. Even with the full contingent of players, only 11 can take the field at once. That means at any given time there are 42 men who are spectators—not participants.

One of the most challenging jobs of the various position coaches is to keep the players who are not on the field focused on the action immediately at hand. If a player can be a vigilant observer and student of the game, he can better prepare himself once his number is called. A good coach knows his players' strengths and weaknesses and will play the best man for the job at any given time. When the coaches can properly coordinate the talents and gifts of their team, they usually see immediate rewards.

In like manner, the Christian life is fully experienced when each of us takes to the field of life using our gifts, talents, interests, and hobbies to the glory of our Lord. Like a good coach, a good pastor will properly assess his congregation and utilize people where they are gifted. An effective Christian is one who knows his or her gifts and seeks the wise counsel of God on how to use them for kingdom work.

The purest form of expression of any gift is when it is expressed with a heart of love and sacrifice toward another person. We should periodically ask ourselves, "Am I using my gifts to honor and glorify God and to uplift other followers?"

Much like a good football team, a church works best when the people work together (participate) for a common good. It's easy to be a spectator. Every Sunday there are millions of fans who sit back and enjoy watching others participate, both in sports and in the ministry of the church. I regularly engage pastors in conversation about the reality that only 10 percent of the congregation does 90 percent of the work—and sometimes 90 percent of the monetary giving as well.

We will be effective as the church of God when each person gets in the game. If we are to make an impact for good, everyone must become involved. I'm reminded of the little boy who volunteered his lunch to Jesus. He was using his gift; Jesus took his offering and multiplied it for everyone's benefit (John 6:1–14). We can all learn something from this young servant's heart:

- God uses what you have to fill a need you never could have filled.

- God uses you where you are to take you where you never could have gone.

- God uses what you can do to accomplish what you never could have done.

- God uses who you are to let you become who you never could have been.

GAME PLAN:

1. Are you in the game or just watching? Ask yourself, "How can God use me today?"

2. Are you studying, observing, and preparing for the time God calls your number and sends you into the game?

ONE OF MY FAVORITE FOOTBALL STORIES UNDERSCORES THE IMPORTANCE OF ENCOURAGEMENT. Motivation often occurs out of the huddle of inspiration. In football, there was probably no greater leader and encourager than Green Bay Hall of Fame quarterback Bart Starr. When he was in his prime there was none better. He utilized his mind and voice to prompt and inspire his team.

While football was a very important part of Starr's life, his family was his central focus. It's interesting to note that many successful football players have a loving and supportive family who encourages and inspires *them* during the tough times.

During the season Starr would try to stay updated with his kids' activities by weekly reviewing their homework and tests. If a paper was particularly good, he would tape a dime to the work and write a note saying, "I love you, and I'm proud of you!"

In 1965 Starr had a bad outing against the St. Louis Cardinals. It was a nationally televised game, and much of America's football audience was watching. The Green Bay quarterback fumbled a few times, and in the final minutes he threw an interception that cost his team the victory. That night the team flew back to Green Bay. Late in the evening he got home only to find a note placed on the refrigerator door. It read, "Dad, I saw your game today. I want you to know I love you, and I'm still proud of you." Signed, Bart Jr.

The words of encouragement from his young son had their influence on Bart, his family, and the Green Bay Packers. He realized the impact that timely comforting remarks could have on a person's perspective.

Articulating an encouraging attitude can motivate people in a special way. Our tongues are but a little muscle, yet they have enormous power for both good and evil. In the book of Proverbs, we find many references dealing with the use of our tongue; for instance, "Reckless words pierce like a sword, but the tongue of the wise brings healing" (12:18), and "He who guards his mouth and his tongue keeps himself from calamity" (21:23).

Merriam-Webster's gives this definition of *encourage*: "To inspire with courage, spirit, or hope." However, encouraging others is counter to what our society projects. Critics and scoffers abound. When we aren't at the top of our game or our business, there are many who will doubt and be cynical. We must remember that Jesus came to encourage us—the Lord came to "SET FREE THOSE WHO ARE OPPRESSED" (Luke 4:18 NASB).

The following is adapted from the writings of Os Hillman. Let's think about how our tongues can be used for encouragement and motivation.

"The tongue has the power of life and death, and those who love it will eat its fruit" (Proverbs 18:21).

Words have the power to motivate or destroy, energize or deflate, inspire or create despair. Many successful executives can remember the time their father failed to give affirmation to them as a child. The result was either overachievement to prove their worth or underachievement to prove he was right.

Many a wife has lost her ability to love because of a critical husband. Many a husband has left a marriage because of words of disrespect and ungratefulness.

In the same way, many an athlete has not performed to his or her ultimate capacity because a coach could not evaluate without attacking the person's character or self-image. Os goes on to say:

> Stories abound regarding the power of words. There are just as many stories of those who have been encouraged, challenged, and comforted with words that made a difference in their lives.
>
> Jesus knew the power of words. He used parables to convey His principles of the kingdom of God. He used words of forgiveness and mercy. He used words to challenge. He used words to inspire His disciples to miraculous faith. [19]

I believe it is especially significant that during Christ's ministry, God chose two critical times to express His encouragement and love for His Son: Jesus' baptism by John (Matthew 3:16–17) and Christ's transfiguration (17:3–5). Both times God said to His only begotten Son, "This is my Son, whom I love; with him I am well pleased."

GAME PLAN:

1. Do your words give life?

2. Do your words inspire and challenge others to greatness?

3. Who does God want you to encourage through your words today? Choose to affirm someone close to you.

IN THE CAPACITY OF A CHAPLAIN AND CHAPEL SPEAKER FOR VARIOUS TEAMS, I often have an opportunity to build a deep, personal relationship with players and coaches. I've had the privilege of working with teams and have seen from the inside the personal challenges many professional athletes face.

One of the growing challenges I've witnessed is the transitioning from being a professional athlete to joining the general working population—it's no easy proposition. I've counseled and known of several athletes who found that transition quite difficult. For many players whose primary identity is in their successes on the field instead of the other traits that distinguish them as a child of God, it is very hard to cope with the chronic pain, lack of intense exercise, testosterone imbalances, and loss of companionship from teammates.

During the 2011 and 2012 seasons we have seen some well-respected players or family members of coaches whose depression ultimately gave way to the extreme act of suicide. The NFL and player representatives are trying to determine if there is a correlation between concussions and depression or if the issues of depression and despair are linked to physiological or psychological roots, or a combination of these factors.

Today, males have a rate of suicide four times greater than females. [20] According to studies, retired NFL players have a higher prevalence of depression than the general population. For many players, succumbing to physical or mental pain is like submitting to your opponent. Hence the expression,

"You need to play hurt." Teams can measure height, weight, jumping ability, speed, strength, bone density, productivity, and endurance. Unfortunately, there is not a good measurement for what a guy struggles with in his quiet moments out of the locker room or spotlight.

As fans we tend to place our favorite athletes on a pedestal that can contribute to the pretense that giving in to physical or mental pain is a sign of weakness. I can think of no greater issue facing many players I've counseled than that of understanding who they are in the sight of God. For those asking the question, "What is my purpose in life?" the answer has to be more than the three-and-a-half years the average player spends in the NFL. The game is important, but it isn't life or death. God has a purpose and plan for each and every one of us.

My experience testifies that for some the issue of coping with life has psychological roots. There may be some things a trained professional Christian psychologist can help a person unpack. For others the root of depression or despair might be associated with a spiritual problem related to fear, anger, a refusal to forgive, feeling unloved, or continual sin. But for many people coping with sadness in their lives, the root of the issue could be chemical. Our DNA, body chemistry, and our inherited predisposition may play an integral part with issues of anxiety and depression. New research shows that things like seasonal affective disorder (SAD) and low Vitamin D, serotonin, norepinephrine, and testosterone levels can contribute to anxiety and depression issues. Even many doctors and pastors now admit that the chemical component of our being can play a part in us appreciating and accepting the love and grace God has given.

As always, God's Word is the ultimate comforter. "Blessed be the God and Father of our Lord Jesus Christ, the Father of mercies and God of all comfort, who comforts us in all our tribulation, that we may be able to comfort those who are in any trouble, with the comfort with which we ourselves are comforted by God" (2 Corinthians 1:3–4 NKJV).

FOOTBALL HAS AFFECTED MY ENTIRE FAMILY'S LIFESTYLE. MY LITTLE BOY CAN'T GO TO BED UNLESS WE GIVE HIM A TWO-MINUTE WARNING.

Dick Vermeil,
Former Kansas City Chiefs Coach

My soul melts from heaviness;
strengthen me according to Your word.
—PSALM 119:28 NKJV

GAME PLAN:

1. Are you, or someone you are close to, experiencing anxiety, depression, or feelings of despair? Have you talked to a doctor, pastor, or close friend?

2. What three things could you do to further explore your feelings and emotions? Just be sure that one of these things is to place them before God in prayer.

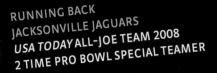

RUNNING BACK
JACKSONVILLE JAGUARS
USA TODAY ALL-JOE TEAM 2008
2 TIME PRO BOWL SPECIAL TEAMER

« FEATURING »

Montell Owens

FAVORITE BIBLE VERSE: MARK 10:31

"But many who are first will be last, and the last first."

From when I was a very young man, I remember my dad coming home after a hard day's work and telling me, "Son, you need to work hard if you're going to make something of yourself." As tired as he was, my dad would work with me, whether it was on the ball field or over homework. My mother would also drag me into the kitchen for one of her many etiquette sessions, first teaching me how to set a table properly, then how to cook and clean.

Growing up in the Northeast Tristate area of Delaware, Pennsylvania, and New Jersey, there were three prevalent things that drove most kids—academics, sports, and the arts. My parents insisted I take advantage of these things, and I found I enjoyed them all. So my life was consumed with studying, playing the trumpet, and practicing various sports.

Unlike some of my buddies who had a great deal of natural ability in these areas, I had to work extra hard at whatever I did. There was no such thing as a free lunch in the Owens' household. My parents loved me a great deal, but regularly reminded me that those who work hard will finish well. Work was not despised but rather was honored by the people of God as good (Proverbs 22:29; 31:13–27; 2 Thessalonians 3:6–12; Proverbs 6:6–11; 10:4–5; Ecclesiastes 10:18). This was true in our household and I wish it were true today in our society.

Today, football is comprised of more than just God-given talent. Those who excel must be fully dedicated to a solid work ethic. In John 4:34–35, Jesus told His disciples that they must also be committed to working hard, "My food is to do the will of Him who sent Me, and to finish His work. Do you not say, 'There are still four months and then comes the harvest'?" (NKJV).

During my tenure at the University of Maine, the emphasis on working hard was underscored by my position coach. Coach Jeff Cole had a poster on his office wall that said, "Every day you either get better or worse, you never stay the same!" And every day Coach Cole would push us a little further to excel in what we did. As a young man who had enough of his domineering attitude, I called home in frustration after a certain football game and told my dad I wanted to quit the team and play elsewhere. Needless to say, my dad quickly reminded me again about developing a character of perseverance because that's a characteristic of a good work ethic too!

During my senior year, I was surprised to be invited to join the Jacksonville Jaguars as an undrafted free agent and, boy, was I excited. But what didn't excite me was seeing that they already had seven other running backs. The coaches saw in me certain things that I could bring to the game—a good work ethic and a heart to keep on keepin' on.

A special team's player needs a heart of a junkyard dog. He needs to keep on keepin' on until the whistle is blown. To be successful, you have to show your opponent that you will not be stopped no matter how many guys they put on you to try and stop you. When you are knocked down, you get back up, and charge forward even harder.

I've been selected to appear in two Pro Bowls so far, and I believe coaches have seen the never-quit attitude I possess. When facing personal challenges and difficult decisions, I try to bring the same conviction and attitude that has allowed me to play football. With the grace of God and understanding His plan for my life, I endeavor to never quit. I rest in God's strength and power, but feel compelled to give it my all in pursuing the goals He has given me.

My heavenly Father and biological father taught me that it isn't what we say but what we do in life that matters. That is one of the principles I've learned from one of the wisest men to ever live on earth—King Solomon.

EVERY YEAR, A FEW DOZEN PROFESSIONAL FOOTBALL PLAYERS FROM EACH CONFERENCE (NATIONAL AND AMERICAN) ARE SELECTED TO COMPETE IN THE PRO BOWL. The starting AFC quarterback for the 2001 Pro Bowl was veteran Rich Gannon of the Oakland Raiders. By the end of the first quarter, Gannon had thrown for 164 yards, including two TDs. His performance testifies to his God-given abilities, mature leadership skills, strength of character, and perseverance. He was unanimously selected as the game's MVP. He repeated that honor in the 2002 Pro Bowl game—a feat matched by no other NFL player.

As we look through the Bible, there are a number of "MVPs" who stand out even more than the great accomplishments of a thousand football stars. Surrounding the remarkable stories and prophecies related to Christ's life is a collection of biblical characters whose lives and testimonies are filled with incidents that depict integrity.

One of my favorite role models is Daniel. The Babylonian captivity set the stage for a truly uncommon display of integrity and valor from Daniel and his three friends. Despite tremendous adversity, they persevered and kept the faith. They trusted God for deliverance and obeyed His commands.

With adversity as a backdrop, Daniel, Shadrach, Meshach, and Abednego developed a godly character that impressed all who observed their struggles. Their main priority was to serve their God with humility, honor, integrity, and fidelity. When King Nebuchadnezzar offered the best food to these committed Jews, they politely refused the enticement that conflicted with God's teachings. Accepting the king's rations and lifestyle would have defiled them, according to Hebrew law. They drew the line and took a stand on biblical principle.

PLAYING QUARTERBACK IS LIKE BEING
IN A STREET FIGHT WITH SIX GUYS,
AND EVERYBODY'S ROOTING FOR THE SIX.

Dan Pastorini,
Former Oilers Quarterback

Daniel and his pals knew that standing on truth would sometimes put a person at odds with those in authority. But they were so committed to being obedient to God's Word, they respectfully declined the king's offers. That is godly character.

When we take a stand for kingdom principles, God's favor is our reward and blessing. For example, "Noah found favor in the eyes of the LORD" and was spared the ravages of the flood (Genesis 6:8 NASB). "Joseph found favor in his sight" (Genesis 39:4 NASB) and was elevated to prominence in Egypt. When Daniel and his associates chose to obey God by not defiling themselves with the king's diet (Daniel 1:8), they demonstrated brave courage and noble integrity.

Today God's favor is the special blessing He grants to His children when we take that difficult stand against the things we know are wrong.

> *No temptation has seized you except what is*
> *common to man. And God is faithful; he will not*
> *let you be tempted beyond what you can bear.*
>
> —1 CORINTHIANS 10:13

GAME PLAN:

1. Are you willing to resist temptation in order to bring glory and honor to God?

2. What are some ways that you can actively prepare for an effective defense that will be needed to resist and overcome temptation?

SORTING THROUGH SOME OF THE DISCOURAG-
ING HEADLINES FROM THE SPORTS SECTION OF
VARIOUS NEWSPAPERS, I find an amazing number of columns
dealing exclusively with the topic of character, or lack thereof.

- Jerry Sandusky, the retired Penn State assistant who coached scores of
  NFL defenders in his three decades at the university, was found guilty
  on 45 counts at his child sex abuse trial. (June 22, 2012)

- NFL Commissioner Goodell suspended Sean Payton, the head coach
  of the Saints, for one year, suspended ringleader and former defensive
  coordinator Gregg Williams indefinitely, suspended New Orleans
  General Manager Mickey Loomis for eight games because of the
  bounty program. (March 22, 2012)

- Lawrence Taylor pleaded guilty to sexual misconduct with a
  16-year-old girl. (May 6, 2010)

- Ben Roethlisberger beats 3rd rape charge and suspended for
  six games. (April 12, 2010)

- Reeling Brett Favre in trouble both on and off the field.
  (October 25, 2010)

- NFL player arrested for DUI in California. (March 27, 2010)

- Local NFL player charged with domestic battery. (April 28, 2010)

  And the list goes on . . . and on . . . and on.

Former NFL Commissioner Paul Tagliabue once stated that there is a "crisis of character in the NFL." Roger Goodell has dealt with his fair share of player issues, too, since taking on the job of NFL Commissioner in 2006. In the spring of 2010, one young player asked Goodell what he considered to be the most important quality for an NFL player. Goodell answered without hesitation. "Well to me," Goodell said, "it starts with character." [21]

NFL teams can't afford to ignore the importance of character when rating the potential of a prospective player. It is more important than terrific times in the 40-yard dash or great moves in the open field.

If we identify fully with what it means to be a true disciple of Christ, if we submit ourselves totally to God's authority over everything, if we humbly wish to serve Him in all our endeavors, then we will find ourselves in direct conflict with Satan. There is no room to compromise with the evil one.

We are either aligned with the kingdom of God and His lordship over our lives, or we are in Satan's kingdom and under his control. It is impossible to serve two masters. We cannot expect to play in the arena with evil elements and effectively work for the Lord. Anyone who possesses spiritual humility will take an uncompromising stand against anything that doesn't glorify Him. To "resist the devil" means "to take a stand against" the person of Satan and anything he represents. It's like former President George W. Bush said regarding terrorism: "Every nation . . . now has a decision to make. Either you are with us, or you are with the terrorists." [22]

Prior to accepting Christ into our lives, we have little power to resist Satan's pull. Our leveling moral influences were societal laws, cultural morals, our upbringing, and those people who influenced our decisions (family, friends, and so forth).

Now, however, as people of deep convictions and having solid faith in Jesus Christ, we have a more powerful influence in our lives—the Holy Spirit. If we draw on God's power to stand firm and resist the temptations that life brings, He will provide a way out for us. I'm reminded of the verse that kept me out of a great deal of trouble in my youth: "No temptation has seized you except what is common to man. And God is faithful; he will not let you be tempted beyond what you can bear. But when you are tempted, he will also provide a way out so that you can stand up under it" (1 Corinthians 10:13).

We are called upon to flee from Satan's influence and humble ourselves before the Lord. Being humble before God doesn't mean being weak before Satan. Just the opposite. Seek the Lord, and He will enable you to stand firm.

Resist the devil and he will flee from you.

—JAMES 4:7 NASB

GAME PLAN:

1. What temptations do you face?

2. Are you humbly seeking God's strength to help you stand firm against those temptations in your daily walk?

I'M REMINDED OF A MOVING STORY ABOUT A SKINNY YOUNG BOY WHO LOVED FOOTBALL WITH ALL HIS HEART. Practice after practice, the boy eagerly gave everything he had to playing the game. But being half the size of the other lads, he got absolutely nowhere. At all the games this hopeful athlete sat on the bench and hardly ever played.

The teenager lived with his father, just the two of them, and they had a special relationship. Even though the son was a bench jockey, his father was always in the stands cheering, never missing a game. The young man was still the smallest in his class when he entered high school.

The father continued to support him, but he also made it very clear that his son did not have to play football if he didn't want to. However, the young man loved the game and decided to hang in there. He was determined to do his best at every practice; perhaps he'd get to play when he became a senior. All through high school he never missed a practice or a game, remaining a benchwarmer all four years. His faithful father remained in the stands, always with words of encouragement.

When the young man went to college, he decided to try out for the football team as a walk-on. Everyone was sure he could never make the cut, but he did. The coach admitted that he kept him on the roster because the young man always put his heart and soul into every practice, and at the same time modeled for his teammates the spirit and hustle they badly needed. The news that he survived the final cut thrilled the young player so much that he rushed to the nearest phone and called his father. His father shared his excitement, and the son sent him season tickets.

As in high school, the persistent young athlete never missed a practice during his four years at college, but he still never played in a game. It was now near the end of his senior football season, and as he trotted onto the practice field shortly before a big playoff game, the coach met him with a telegram. The young man read the message and became deathly silent. Swallowing hard, he mumbled to the coach, "My father died this morning. Is it all right if I miss practice today?" The coach put his arm gently around his shoulders and said, "Take the rest of the week off, son. And don't even plan to come back for the game on Saturday."

Saturday arrived, and the game was not going well. In the third quarter, when the team was ten points behind, a silent young man quietly slipped into the empty locker room and put on his football gear. As he ran onto the sidelines, the coach and his players were astonished to see their faithful teammate back so soon.

"Coach, please let me play. I've just got to play today," said the young man. The coach pretended not to hear him; there was no way he wanted his worst player in this close playoff game. But the young man persisted, and finally, feeling sorry for the kid, the coach gave in. "All right," he said. "You can go in." Before long, the coach, the players, and everyone in the stands couldn't believe their eyes.

The little unknown player, who had never played in a sanctioned game, was doing everything right. He ran, passed, blocked, and tackled like a star, and his team began to triumph—the score was soon tied. In the closing seconds of the game, the young man intercepted a pass and ran it back for the winning touchdown.

The fans broke loose, his teammates hoisted him onto their shoulders—such cheering you've never heard. Finally, after the stands had emptied and the team had showered and left the locker room, the coach noticed the young man sitting quietly alone in the corner. The coach came to him and said, "Kid, I can't believe it. You were fantastic! Tell me, what got into you? How did you do it?" The young man looked at the coach, with tears in his eyes, and said, "Well, you knew my dad died, but did you know that he was blind?" He swallowed hard and forced a smile. "Dad came to all my games, but today was the first time he could see me play, and I wanted to show him I could do it!"

Like this athlete's father, God is always there cheering for us, always reminding us to go on. He's even offering us His hand, for He knows what is best and is willing to give us what we need and not simply what we want. God has never missed a single game. What a joy to know that life is meaningful if lived for the highest goal. Live for *Him*; He's watching and helping us in the game of life!

GAME PLAN:

1. Do you live your life as if your heavenly Father is watching you all of the time?

2. In your daily walk, strive to make choices that honor and glorify God. What is one thing that immediately comes to mind that you can change?

I GREW UP IN AN AREA OF EAST OAKLAND WHERE MOST OF THE KIDS IN MY NEIGHBOR-HOOD COULD RUN FAST.

I was very gangly, with legs like stilts, so speed was something I could only dream about. I didn't have the flat-out quickness of my friends, but I learned to compensate. Early in my limited football experience as a receiver, I realized that there was more than one way to get open. Deception and trickery often worked. My fakes and jukes would create separation between the speedy coverage men and me. This would allow me to make strategic catches.

It's no secret why players like Ed McCaffrey of the Denver Broncos have been so successful. McCaffrey not only used a tremendous work ethic, great hands, precise patterns, and a desire to perfect his position, but he was also unbelievably deceptive. While not as fast as most receivers, he used deception (fakes) to fool the cornerbacks assigned to cover him. Ed McCaffrey amazed fans with acrobatic catches and amazing stamina until his retirement in 2003.

The great Indiana Colts receiver Wes Welker is another guy who can put the moves on people. With any great receiver, a fake could be as simple as a head bob in one direction, a short cut in the opposite direction they intend to go, or pretending to catch a throw that hasn't even been made. Anything that will throw off the pace and speed of the defender will aid the receiver in getting separation. While deceptions work well for a receiver, in the Word of God we are cautioned to be on the lookout for "fakes." We are constantly being faced with fakes of one kind or another. Unless you live in a box, you will encounter those who are charlatans and deceivers. They are quick to win your trust and confidence only to take advantage of your gracious generosity or kindness.

Many folks seeking to find hope and assurance buy into the advertisements from an assortment of psychics, astrologers, and soothsayers who do not rely on Christ as their Lord. The Bible warns us against these "false prophets" who are demon-driven and full of trickery.

We are cautioned not to fall into the trap of thinking that the teachings of these false prophets is harmless. Many Hollywood personalities and some very visible NFL players who endorse things like crystals, tarot cards, palm reading, or other such trickery find it reassuring to share their "readings" with an audience. But Scripture is clear about believing in such things or even spending time with these cultic tools: "Do not be carried away by all kinds of strange teachings" (Hebrews 13:9).

The above practices are not harmless. They have the potential to creep into our thoughts and attitudes. These "fakes" and their deviant teachings can direct our resources and attention onto things that ultimately lead to evil. Even some "religious leaders" are not exempt from being deceitful. They take Scripture out of context and lead their innocent followers into believing that they have mystical powers. Leaders like Guyana's Jim Jones or Waco's David Koresh are examples of how cults can capture the heart, imagination, hope, and finances of unsuspecting individuals.

In Rita McKenzie Fisher's book titled *Lessons from the Gridiron*, she describes some ways we can test a person to be sure we are not being "faked out":

> Do they merely use the name of Jesus or do they truly honor Him? Is salvation only through Christ or by their own divine nature? Do they add "new revelations" from God or do they rely on His Word as

written? Are they open and honest or exclusive and secretive? Is their loyalty to Jesus or to the group leader? Do they publicize financial statements or keep records secret? Are the leader's views the only ones accepted or can you read the Bible and pray out loud by yourself?

If you receive incorrect answers to these questions, beware! Watch out for "fakes"—they will push you out of position for catching the truth.

"I am sending you out like sheep among wolves. Therefore be as shrewd as snakes and as innocent as doves."
—MATTHEW 10:16

GAME PLAN:

1. Are you easily influenced by fakes? Remember always to compare the words of men to the Word of God.

2. Read 2 John (the entire book is only 13 verses). Pray that God will give you wisdom as you seek to follow pastors and teachers who are well grounded in the truth of the Bible.

IN 1936, SLINGIN' SAMMY BAUGH WAS RATED THE FINEST COLLEGE FOOTBALL PLAYER IN THE COUNTRY. Baugh didn't disappoint the owner of the Washington Redskins, George Preston Marshall, who drafted him as a first-round pick. As a professional player, Baugh went on to set several offensive records, some of which have never been toppled, even by the greats of our day.

Sammy played 16 seasons with the Redskins. This was before facemasks, high-tech protective gear, and personal trainers. At 38, he was still calling plays and performing at a high level. But after years of battling rushing linemen, Baugh's long, gaunt frame showed ample fatigue and scarring.

In 1952, Baugh and his team lined up against their rivals, the Chicago Cardinals. They were facing a fearsome front four and a hostile Comiskey Park crowd. Time and again Sammy left the protective pocket to complete passes over a frustrated Cardinal defense. Despite a preseason injury to his throwing hand, Baugh's bullet-like passes screamed through the outstretched hands of defensive linemen.

Finally an exasperated Cardinal tackle named Don Joyce had had enough. He ran into the unprotected quarterback and decked him. In a reactive manner, Sammy threw a punch with his legendary right hand. The fight lasted long enough to get both players ejected from the game. That was the last time Sammy Baugh cocked his right arm on a football field. He retired and went on to become a successful assistant coach.

What separated Slingin' Sammy from other passers that came along after him was that he was an original—the real deal. He was to the quarterback position what Henry Ford was to the Model T. Others had invented the forward pass, but Baugh was the first one to make full use of it. He perfected various formations to take advantage of his accuracy and delivery.

Baugh used his God-given talents and abilities to the fullest. A smart player recognizes his strengths and weaknesses so he can maximize his potential and also allows the coach's instruction to live through him. Sammy was very coachable and teachable. His college and professional coaches spoke confidence and assurance into his life and into his play. They were his mentors, and he duplicated their instruction in his daily workouts and game situations. But Sammy was a team player. He recognized that even though the quarterback was important, so was every member of the team—and they could only win when the entire team pulled together.

In like manner, God wants every Christian to understand his or her spiritual gifts and use them wisely and in conjunction with others. According to 1 Corinthians 12 and Romans 12, once we accept Christ into our hearts, God gives us our spiritual gifts—the methods through which the Holy Spirit ministers to others (1 Corinthians 12:11). Gifts can manifest themselves in a desire and ability to teach, preach, serve, encourage, counsel, sing, administer a program, or other such expressions of service. It is clear that the Holy Spirit empowers the abilities and talents of people so as to speak through them, much in the same way a coach will speak through a good player.

Unlike our football analogy, it would be inaccurate to equate a natural ability with a spiritual gift; the apostle Paul illustrated the difference. He could have used his knowledge of philosophy, language, and literature to write and speak great messages. Instead, he said, "I did not come with superiority of speech or of wisdom, proclaiming to you the testimony of God. For I determined to know nothing among you except Jesus Christ, and Him crucified" (1 Corinthians 2:1–2 NASB).

We are encouraged in Scripture not to sit on our spiritual gifts. Peter said this concerning our abilities:

> As each one has received a special gift, employ it in serving one another as good stewards of the manifold grace of God. Whoever speaks, is to do so as one who is speaking the utterances of God; whoever serves is to do so as one who is serving by the strength which God supplies; so that in all things God may be glorified through Jesus Christ. (1 Peter 4:10–11 NASB)

We must use our gifts to God's glory.

But to each one is given the manifestation of the Spirit for the common good.
—1 CORINTHIANS 12:7 NASB

GAME PLAN:

1. What gifts are you using to advance the kingdom of God?

2. How can you use your gifts more effectively in your Christian testimony among your family, friends, and coworkers?

42 ЯUП, ВАВУ, ЯUП

IT WAS A COOL FALL AFTERNOON IN 1994 AT THE
UNIVERSITY OF WASHINGTON FOOTBALL STADIUM—
THE BEGINNING OF ANOTHER SEASON. One of the best
college running backs of all time was poised to take the field for his last year.
The legendary "tunnel" leading to the field was electrified with tension as
Napoleon Kaufman and his teammates stood and contemplated the game
and their futures. Just two weeks prior to that moment, as a confused young
man, Kaufman had been in a street fight after a night of clubbing and drinking. Napoleon recalled, "It was all about me. My world consisted of acting
like a fool so that others would recognize me. I was living a life built on external rewards that I thought would make me happy. In my heart, I knew I was
living a lie."

Known as "Nip" to his teammates, he remembered wondering if he
could get through that first game. Doctors had worked hours to try to recon-
struct his eye socket due to the injury suffered in the street brawl. His
physician had advised him to give up football due to the fragile nature of the
screws that were placed in his head during surgery.

"That season was difficult, as I was filled with fear and worry," Kaufman
said. "I was constantly trying to meet everyone's expectations while feeling
that I could fumble at any time. Being one of the smallest players in the
game, I often felt threatened."

Kaufman finished the season, and over his collegiate career led the Pac-10 with 4,041 rushing yards and set numerous Washington Huskies records. He did so well his name was placed in contention for the coveted Heisman and Doak Walker awards. In the spring of 1995, he was the first-round draft pick of the Oakland Raiders.

Despite his success, inwardly Kaufman knew that his life was a mess. His arrogant attitude and foul mouth baited others to confrontation. He showed disrespect to players by placing his primary focus on his personal accomplishments and scores. But inside he was struggling. His precious new bride beckoned him to be a leader at home. His teammates encouraged him to "quit actin' a fool." Through a series of events both on and off the field he felt that "God was trying to tell him something." People began sending him Christian books; strangers began coming up to him and saying things like, "God has a plan for you. He wants to use your life for kingdom work."

Kaufman knew that in the past pro athletes were known and admired for being *record breakers*, and he realized that many of today's athletes are known for being *lawbreakers*. He didn't want to end up an embarrassment to himself, to his family, or to God. Kaufman recalls a conversation he had with fullback Jerome Davidson who impressed him with the grace and peace that only a life in Christ can bring.

That night Kaufman gave his life to Jesus. Both he and his wife, Nicole, were baptized and motivated to study God's Word. Instead of focusing on himself, he now focuses upon God's plan for his life. Instead of being an embarrassment to the team, he has become a role model. Instead of worrying about external rewards, he now places his attention on the internal blessings that come with a dedicated life.

Kaufman now sees trials as a testing ground for his faith. He agrees with James (the half-brother of Christ): "Consider it pure joy, my brothers, whenever you face trials of many kinds, because you know that the testing of your faith develops perseverance. Perseverance must finish its work so that you may be mature and complete, not lacking anything" (James 1:2–4).

And, like the psalmist, Kaufman constantly remembers that during the fearful times, "I will fear no evil, for you are with me" (Psalm 23:4).

Kaufman's best seasons came after he accepted Christ into his heart; in 1997–98, he rushed for 1,294 yards. His quickness and superior decision-making skills propelled him to become one of the most outstanding running backs in the NFL. He and Nicole now have three sons and one daughter and are engaged in an exciting ministry called "Crucified with Christ." Nip also serves as the Raiders' team chaplain.

So I sought for a man among them who would . . . stand in the gap before Me.

—EZEKIEL 22:30 NKJV

GAME PLAN:

1. When you encounter trials in your life, do you see them as a way to deepen and strengthen your walk with God?

2. As you walk through difficult times, remember to call out to Jesus, ask for the comfort and peace that only He can give.

CHARLIE TATE, FORMER COACH WITH THE UNIVERSITY OF MIAMI, TELLS US, "HAVING A PRO OFFENSE . . . with great receivers but no first-rate quarterback is like having a new limousine with a chimpanzee at the wheel." [23] But what makes a great quarterback?

The majority of decisions made by a quarterback occur in 3-second intervals. That is the time a passer usually has from the moment he takes the snap from the center, hurries back a few yards, searches for a receiver, and fires the ball at a moving target.

To be consistently successful at this day after day and to compete at the NFL level, a quarterback needs several skills and talents. Certainly having a strong and accurate arm is important—he must be able to fling the ball from various positions and for distances up to 60 or 70 yards. He also must have good rhythm and footwork to avoid those blitzing linebackers and safeties. Most quarterbacks who last more than a few years are nimble and agile when it comes to scampering away from trouble. Good footwork is about rhythm and selected movement. Having the right balance and dexterity are key to being effective in gaining more time through scrambling.

A good sense of timing is also critical. My friend Rich Gannon told me, "You've got to have a game clock going in your head. Everything you do must be totally reactive because you just don't have the time to really think things through during the heat of the battle."

Decision-making is another key. When you think about the great NFL quarterbacks, you don't necessarily think about a big, powerful quarterback who can chuck the ball a mile. No, you think of a good decision maker—a guy who can call the right play at the right time, a guy who can anticipate and

make quick adjustments to compensate for the defensive play of his opponent.

Finally, an NFL quarterback needs to be a leader. Someone once said, "Leaders are not those who strive to be first but those who are first to strive and who give their all for the success of the team. True leaders are first to see the need, envision the plan, and empower the team for action. By the strength of the leader's commitment, the power of the team is unleashed."

When you see a team struggling, it is most likely because there is a lack of good leadership in some facet of the game. Any championship team has outstanding men who can step up and take on the leadership role—they become field generals. Marian Anderson—the acclaimed African-American singer—once said, "Leadership should be born out of the understanding of the needs of those who would be affected by it." [24]

Perhaps the single most important trait of a great quarterback and a great man of God is knowing the hearts of the people he is leading. It is a wise football player and servant of God who shows compassion and displays understanding. A person will generate enormous effort when he knows he is respected, loved, and cared for.

Scripture calls men to be leaders in our homes, in our workplaces, and in our churches. To be leaders we must first test our own hearts for purity, righteousness, and obedience. Then we must be willing and fit to lead by example and model the principles of God's Word.

Be a leader, my friend.

TEXAS STADIUM HAS A HOLE IN
ITS ROOF SO GOD CAN WATCH
HIS FAVORITE TEAM PLAY.

D. D. Lewis,
Former Cowboy Linebacker

*"If anyone wants to be first, he must be
the very last, and the servant of all."*
—MARK 9:35

GAME
PLAN:

1. Are you an effective leader
for your family, in your workplace,
and in your church?

2. First Corinthians 9:19–27 discusses Paul's
motivation for his leadership of the early
church. As a leader, are you willing to
humble yourself in service to others so
that they may come to know the Lord?

THE TITLE OF A FEATURED ARTICLE IN THE JANUARY 8, 2001, issue of *Christianity Today* is "The Glory of the Ordinary." This interesting interview of quarterback Trent Dilfer by Jeff Sellers provides keen insights into the controversy (and sometimes hypocrisy) associated with Christian football players.

Dilfer was drafted by the Tampa Bay Buccaneers as the sixth player selected from the highly touted class of 1994. The Bucs had high expectations for the 6'4", 229-pound rookie, and after working through some difficult times, Dilfer eventually led the young franchise to a playoff spot in the 1997 season. Unfortunately, his 1998 campaign was below par, and the Bucs decided to place him in a backup role to Shaun King of Tulane. Finally, in 1999, Tampa Bay traded the inconsistent Dilfer to the Baltimore Ravens.

The uncertainty of his status (he worked in a backup role to Tony Banks) and the problems of dealing with an injured knee began to wear on Dilfer's spirit. However, even with all the possibility for discouragement, he remained strong and dedicated to the game and to his faith.

As a mature believer, Dilfer has a tremendous sense of humility and perspective in knowing how football fits into the scheme of things: "I'm not a football player who happens to do Christianity. I'm a Christian that just happens to be an NFL player," he says. His observations of many Christian athletes in the league is that, just like in the real world, there is a significant difference between those who are truly committed to the principles of their faith and those who just wish to give a "nod to God." [25]

In his quest to land a starting position, Dilfer prayed that the Holy Spirit would allow him to have an attitude of joy and peace in the midst of his setbacks. During even this challenging time he wanted to be used by God to encourage others on his team who were going through their own difficulties.

Throughout the 2000 season Dilfer continued to back up the struggling Tony Banks. Midway through the season, Coach Brian Billick had had enough. Playoff hopes were forming, and he needed a quarterback who could lead the Ravens to a berth in the Super Bowl. Dilfer got his shot to perform.

To most critics' amazement, Dilfer went on to lead the Ravens to an exciting victory in Super Bowl XXXV. In an industry that is laden with big egos, Dilfer makes genuine humility one of his top spiritual quests, as demonstrated in his post-game interview. His words were indicative of what he had written earlier in his prayer journal: "Thank you, God, that you are using football as the means to break me so that I may know you better." [26]

Despite his success both on and off the field, Dilfer knows a player's faith doesn't guarantee a winning season. He said, "I don't think that our success level dictates the amount we can glorify God." He maintains, "God calls believers first to be faithful, and secondarily to develop 100 percent of what He has given them—whether they are athletes, business owners, spouses, parents, or in any other vocation." [27]

During his *Christianity Today* interview with Jeff Sellers, Dilfer went on to say, "It's the process more than the product that brings [God] glory. When folks are truly searching and looking into people's lives to find answers, where they'll see God is in a consistent life and in the process, not necessarily the end result or the product." [28]

Dilfer realizes the hypocrisy of some who, when winning, will stand before the national media to proclaim their Lord, then turn right around and become involved with immoral or illegal activities that dishonor God. This is why Dilfer feels that consistency in a faithful walk is something for which each believer should strive: "I believe that I am more motivated professionally than I've ever been because God has given me a certain amount of ability, leadership, and other areas that I am called to develop through His strength. This will naturally help me progress in a successful way." [29]

God has given each man in the NFL unique and special talents that make them football players, but choosing football as an occupation should not preclude their serving and honoring God. Dilfer said, "It's a time where God has pulled together a group of men to say, 'Okay, after all that's just been said and done, what is our purpose and what is our perspective on life?'" [30]

Christian athletes who are sincere in their faith will tell you that their praises to God after a hard-fought game are a "natural expression of core beliefs" that guide their daily lives. Dilfer's game-day prayer is always the same: "I need your Spirit to be in total control of my thoughts, actions, emotions, and words." [31] This is a reminder to all of us as to how we should place God at the center of all that we do.

GAME PLAN:

1. Do you allow God to be in control of your words, thoughts, and actions?

2. We all need encouragement to keep our focus on God daily so that we can glorify and honor Him through our words, thoughts, and actions. How can you be an encouragement to a fellow believer?

« FEATURING »

Danny Wuerffel

FAVORITE BIBLE VERSE: 2 CORINTHIANS 4:18

So we fix our eyes not on what is seen, but on what is unseen.
For what is seen is temporary, but what is unseen is eternal.

After retiring from football in 2004, I elected to leave the world of the NFL and focus my energies and attention on serving the poor in the Ninth Ward of New Orleans through Desire Street Ministries (DSM). I became the Executive Director after Hurricane Katrina, and now the new DSM serves urban ministry leaders all over the Southeast. I've been excited to see the recent success of my friend and fellow Gator, Tim Tebow. At a time in this nation when we seem to have lost decorum and respect, it is important to me to see mature athletes respectfully interact with community—especially teammates, family, and those people who look up to us. For that very reason, it was a special honor that, in 2005, the All Sports Association of Fort Walton Beach created the Wuerffel Trophy to be awarded annually to the college player who best exemplified great character, good academics, outstanding play on the field, and provided service to their community. In 2009, I presented that trophy to Tim Tebow.

I really admire how Tim uses his platform in such a positive way. I believe there is no right way for evangelical players to use the platform of football. It's really up to the individual. I chose to subtly fold my hands in prayer after a big moment. I'm really amused about all the media hype that happens when committed Christian men express their celebration by demonstrating a humble spirit through kneeling in prayer or pointing to God.

Also important to me is how we as Christians deal with the struggles life will bring to each of us. Football, like other professions, has its hard knocks and personal challenges. The struggles I faced in football helped me in June 2011 when I was diagnosed with Guillain-Barre Syndrome, a disorder of unknown origin that turns the body's immune system against the nervous system. This results in partial paralysis and prolonged muscle weakness until the body can recover.

As I fight this disease, I'm reminded of the battles each of us face every day in defending our faith and standing up for what's right. The Lord reminds us: "Peace I leave with you, My peace I give to you; not as the world gives do I give to you. Let not your heart be troubled, neither let it be afraid" (John 14:27 NKJV).

> For the LORD loves the just and
> will not forsake his faithful ones.
> They will be protected forever.
> —PSALM 37:28

AS THE FRESH FRAGRANCE OF THE EVENING DEW SETTLES UPON THE RIVER SHORELINE OUTSIDE MY WINDOW, I'M REMINDED THAT AUTUMN IS NOT FAR OFF. The surrounding forest with its majestic deciduous trees becomes an easel for God to display His artistic craftsmanship by painting an array of fall colors throughout the landscape.

This is also a time when avid fans are getting ready for some serious *football*! While teams are finalizing their preseason workouts and trimming their rosters, millions of viewers prepare their living rooms and dens for the weekly event.

For an armchair quarterback, there is usually a ritual associated with preparing for the season. A fresh start is important. The fishing equipment is stored until next spring, the "honey-do list" gets caught up, clutter from under the easy chair is vacuumed away, fresh batteries are placed in the remote control, and plenty of popcorn is purchased.

Often Dad will enlist the help of his kids to get the yard in order for the long winter so that routine chores are limited—allowing more time to watch football. Of course, these duties are accomplished a great deal quicker when everyone pitches in. We remind our kids that by working diligently together we can accomplish much. We call this togetherness *teamwork*.

Even the casual observer of the game will probably hear more talk about teamwork than any other topic. The most successful families and teams are the ones whose participants understand how to work together effectively in accomplishing their goals.

Starting with the first mini-camp and leading to the pep talk by the head coach before every game, players will hear about the importance of working together—being on the same page. Having an unselfish heart and being an encouragement to others is something that is difficult to coach. Pride, jealousy, envy, and strife are part of humanity's fallen nature.

If the linemen don't sacrificially give of their bodies to block their assigned player, even All-Pro running backs have little chance of gaining yardage. *Webster's New World College Dictionary* defines teamwork as "joint action by a group of people, in which individual interests are subordinated to group unity and efficiency; coordinated effort, as of an athletic team."

Such was the case with Paul's agricultural illustration in 1 Corinthians 3. Paul (the one planting) and his faithful partner in ministry, Apollos (the one watering), had their God-appointed work. As an evangelist it was essential for Paul to plant the seeds of hope, love, peace, joy, and salvation among those he contacted. He needed the further teaching and encouragement of someone like Apollos to begin "watering" the seeds of knowledge so that people would grow in their faith and obedience to Christ Jesus.

Paul reminded us, "Now to each one the manifestation of the Spirit is given for the common good. . . . All these are the work of one and the same Spirit, and he gives them to each one, just as he determines" (1 Corinthians 12:7, 11).

Committed believers who are obedient to God's leading recognize that we are all part of one team—God's. We work together as sowers, planters, waterers, and harvesters to encourage people to consider the claims of Jesus.

Scripture reminds us that none should look upon their kingdom work with pride or conceit. God calls us to be humble of heart, sacrificing for the good of others. Jesus was the ultimate example of this (Philippians 2:5–8), and the supreme demonstration of humility is when we imitate Him: "We know love by this, that He laid down His life for us; and we ought to lay down our lives for the brethren" (1 John 3:16 NASB).

Let's remember that it's not about being important but rather doing what is important. Just as with Paul and Apollos, if we don't worry about who gets the credit we will participate in many team victories.

He who plants and he who waters are one;
but each will receive his own reward according
to his own labor. For we are God's fellow workers.

—1 CORINTHIANS 3:8–9 NASB

GAME PLAN:

1. Have you identified your position on God's team? Are you a sower, planter, waterer, or harvester? Take time to pray and ask God to reveal to you how you can be most effective for the advancement of His kingdom.

2. How can you help the other members of your "team"—at the workplace, at home, or at church?

THE MIND IS A POWERFUL THING AND GREATLY INFLUENCES OUR BEHAVIOR FOR GOOD OR FOR EVIL. The legendary Alabama coach, Paul Bear Bryant, told of a unique moment in Bama history when, with 2 minutes remaining in a critical game against their rival, a miracle of the mind happened.

Alabama was first and ten on the opponent's 20-yard line. They had a 5-point lead with no timeouts remaining for either team. Bryant's starting quarterback took the ball on a quarterback sneak and was hit hard—his pain was such that he had to remove himself from the game. Coach Bryant found his rookie backup quarterback and told him the following: "This game is ours if you do what I say. I want you to rush the ball all three remaining downs. Do *not*, under any circumstance, put it up in the air. Even if we don't make a first down, there will be so little time left on the clock that our defense will hold them until the game is over." The coach focused his gaze and said, "Do you understand?" With a big gulp the young man responded, "Yes, sir, I understand: don't put the ball in the air."

The rookie ran onto the field and immediately called an off-tackle play that gained no yards. On the third down, he executed a sneak and gained 1 yard. On the last down, with just seconds remaining in the game, the nervous quarterback once again called an off-tackle play. This time the running back missed the handoff, leaving the ball in the quarterback's hands. The frightened rookie looked up to see his tight end frantically waving his arms in the end zone. He was wide open. The quarterback knew that all he had to do was lob a pass and the game was over.

What he didn't know was that an All-American safety had let the tight end roam free, hoping the quarterback would throw in that direction. The safety had lightning-quick speed and planned to intercept the ball.

As the pass was released, the safety moved toward it with the speed and grace of a cheetah. The talented defensive back grabbed the spiraling ball and began his journey, 100 yards to Bama's end zone.

The rookie quarterback was the only person who had a chance to tackle the elusive defender. He chased the safety down the field and finally tackled him on his own 2-yard line just as the whistle blew, ending the game.

As the game ended, the two coaches met in the center of the field to exchange handshakes. The perplexed coach of the opposing team asked Coach Bryant, "According to our scouting reports, your rookie quarterback isn't very swift on his feet. How on earth did he catch our guy—one of the quickest in college football?"

With that famous southern accent, Coach Bryant drawled, "Your man was running for six points. My man was running for his life!" [32]

Yes, our minds affect our actions. Just as that young quarterback set out to follow the coach's instructions, when faced with the realities and temptations on the field, he took another path—one that was almost disastrous. In life, we can have the best intentions of doing what we know is right, but if our mind is undisciplined we can be tempted to do evil. God's Word tells us to be *single-minded* in purpose and intent. We are to focus our thoughts on things that are pure, truthful, admirable, noble, and of good character. If our minds are disciplined we will be less likely to give way to temptation or to worry. With a disciplined mind we will enjoy a more peaceful life.

Our mind can't focus on two things at once. If our attention is on those things that bring honor to God and to our family, we will be less likely to have fear, worry, and temptation rule our actions. Remember, we are fighting a spiritual battle. Paul reminded us that we need to develop a stronghold of faith and of thought to conquer temptation: "For our struggle is not against flesh and blood, but against the rulers, against the authorities, against the powers of this dark world and against the spiritual forces of evil in the heavenly realms" (Ephesians 6:12).

God's Word tells us to choose our thoughts. By surrendering our desires and our will, the Holy Spirit will help guide our attitudes and actions. Only the power of God can help us overcome the daily temptations life brings (2 Corinthians 10:3–5) and help us avoid disaster. If we truly wish to change the way we live, we need to change the way we think.

> *You were taught, with regard to your former way of life, to put off your old self, which is being corrupted by its deceitful desires; to be made new in the attitude of your minds.*
>
> —EPHESIANS 4:22–23

GAME PLAN:

1. Sometimes we know what we are supposed to do as followers of Christ, yet we do not do it, just as Paul confessed in Romans 7:15. Ask God to strengthen you in your fight against these temptations.

2. Are there particular areas in your life where—despite your best intentions—you are not following God's will? Ask a godly friend or pastor to help you be accountable and keep you on the right path.

FOOTBALL HAS LONG BEEN CONSIDERED THE GAME OF LIFE BY MANY PHILOSOPHICALLY DRIVEN PERSONALITIES. From his experiences with the game as a young athlete, Dr. Larry Wilhite, a management consultant, would attest to that theory. [33]

His first time playing organized football came when he was a freshman in high school. He attended a small school in Idaho that had an enrollment of about 100 students. There were only about 25 boys eligible for varsity football—most with little talent beyond being able to fog a mirror during a physical exam.

Larry was naturally big—as a freshman he weighed 220 pounds and stood over 6 feet tall. As usual, that summer he bucked hay bales for his uncle and developed muscles where most kids only dreamed of having them. In fact, he had a reputation: people called him the "Human Haying Machine." Fortunately for him, and possibly others, he was clueless about his physical attributes. He was just like any other kid his age—he wanted to look like someone else and he wanted to be someone else. Larry turned out for the varsity team and began preseason conditioning. The small contingent of players called it "practice."

Given the brutal nature of the sport and the few players the coach had to choose from, Larry had to be a welcome sight. However, he knew little about football. The only thing this big guy knew was that he had to make the team or suffer great personal disappointment and embarrassment among his friends and family who encouraged him to play.

Practice went on for a week, and Larry loved it—he was a very coachable kid. He hung on every word the coach uttered and made every effort to impress the team with his attitude and enthusiasm. If the coach said jump, Larry asked how high on the way up. In everything the freshman did, he

doubled his effort in an attempt to be what the coach wanted him to be.

As practice continued, the philosophy of the experience began to sink in. Larry was impressed with what the coaches were telling him: "The first hit of the game is the most important. Hit the other guy harder and more times than he hits you. Do your job better than the other guy 85 percent of the time, and you will win!" It made a lot of sense.

As the team was beginning to get the flow of the game, the coach began to talk about the pain and sacrifice required to play football. It seemed to the team that he was developing their courage so that they wouldn't be fearful. Due to the limited number of players, the coach told them, "Be prepared to play hurt." Larry understood the concept. He was confident and anxious to proceed.

Finally it came time to pass out equipment. The poor school district had little or no athletic budget so most of the equipment consisted of hand-me-downs from larger school districts. To make matters worse, the freshmen were the last to get their gear.

Everything about Larry's uniform was wrong. If an item was supposed to fit tight, it fit loose. If an item was to fit loose, it fit tight. His shoulder pads were half the size he needed and the helmet was too big for his head—it wobbled when he ran. Given the nature of the game and the condition of the equipment, it was a good bet that sometime during the season most of the players were going to get hurt.

Game day finally arrived, and the big freshman was quite a sight. If a cartoonist were to sketch him, he would have looked like two humps on a camel with a large bombardier helmet in the middle. But there he was, a starter on the varsity squad, playing both offense and defense. As Larry stepped onto the field his mind began to rush with the coach's challenges: "Hit first, hit hard, hit often, and be prepared to play hurt."

The game began with a flurry. The first play on offense was called over

Larry's tackle position. He sized up the guy across the "trench" and felt confident that he could take him. The ball was snapped, and he fired off from his stance like a cannonball. There was a huge collision, a big pile of humanity stacked up on the 30-yard line in a cloud of dust, and Larry was somewhere in the middle.

As the pile began to unfold, something was wrong. Larry suddenly realized he must be hurt. The coach's words welled up in him. He managed to get up, but had great difficulty seeing. His left eye was blind, and he had tunnel vision in the right. One of the seniors grabbed the wobbly freshman and got him into the next play. Larry appeared to be injured, but he was playing. Somehow he managed to work his way back to his team's side of the field, and then he heard it. The coach yelled, *Wilhite! Turn your helmet around. You're looking through the ear hole!*

Larry learned a great deal about football that day, some of it a little embarrassing. He learned an important thing about life, too: attitude has a lot to do with *how* you do.

In life, just as in football, we win with the right attitude, and everyone we touch on any given day wins by how we act and react toward them. So on the first play of each day, project your best attitude, sustain it at least 85 percent of the time, and even when you "gotta play hurt," do it with a good attitude. When you do, you win, and everyone else wins too!

GAME PLAN:

1. As you get up and prepare for your day, ask God to give you the confidence you need to act and react in a manner glorifying to Him regardless of what circumstances you encounter.

2. As you greet people this day, remember that you may be the only "Bible" some people will ever see. Make sure you are one they want to learn more about.

CAN YOU IMAGINE A HIGH SCHOOL SENIOR RUNNING 3,166 YARDS AND SCORING 54 TOUCHDOWNS IN ONE SEASON? Think about accumulating enough yardage as a high school player to be placed in the record books as Top 10 prep of all time. Despite the fact that his mom and dad went through a tough divorce when he was eleven, and he and his brother lived with their mom in a two-bedroom apartment in a government housing project, Shaun Alexander made something of his life.

As an All-American prep star Shaun was named "Mr. Football" or "Alexander the Great" as he graduated from Boone County High School. But he wasn't finished with the game. While many colleges were interested in Shaun, he picked the University of Alabama Crimson Tide backfield as his home for the next four years. He left Alabama holding 15 records, including 3,565 career rushing yards.

In 2000, the Seattle Seahawks drafted Alexander where he was known for his speed, agility, and explosive power. When a few middle linebackers were asked about who was one of the toughest guys to stop, Shaun Alexander's name was usually mentioned as a "train wreck" for opposing lineman and linebackers to take on. He was a fierce competitor and racked up over 9,453 rushing yards and 1,520 receiving yards as he spent his last year with the Washington Redskins. It is a fitting number for a good running back to retire with exactly 100 rushing touchdowns.

After nine hard-fought seasons many NFL players would take their NFL pension and live a life of luxury playing golf, fishing, hunting, and enjoying the beaches of Hawaii. This was not the life God called Shaun to savor. He and his family started the Shaun Alexander Foundation, a non-profit organization that inspires kids to stay in school, strive for educational excellence, and plan their futures. It is amazing to think that a day after scoring 2 touchdowns to lead the Seahawks (winners over the Carolina Panthers 34–14) to the first Super Bowl appearance in their 30-year history, Alexander returned to Madrona Elementary School in Seattle to hand out the prizes at a special chess tournament organized by America's Foundation for Chess (AF4C).

The strategic thinking that allows Shaun to compete as a chess champion and a professional football player is the kind of focus he has brought into ministry. Shaun has a great testimony and character because he has learned the importance of walking with God. In his book, *The Walk*, Shaun describes the importance of knowing God in a deep and personal way. His life and book is based upon the words the Holy Spirit gave him, "This is what happens when you walk the Walk. Not perfection. I'm not looking for perfection. I'm looking for order."

Shaun reminds us of a biblical hero named Enoch. He was a man who never died. According to Scripture he was translated, taken alive, to heaven after he "walked with God" for three hundred years (Genesis 5:22). The Bible also refers to others who regularly took the time to "walk with God." Men such as Noah, Abraham, Jacob, and Moses spent time focusing on God's plan for their lives. They prayed, mediated, listened, and talked with God.

As we live out our hectic pace in this crazy world, most people don't take the time to even read their Bible or have a real devotional time with God. According to a study Jack Hayford did on prayer, many pastors spend less than twelve minutes a day in prayer. [34] The October 2012 *Baptist Press News* also affirms that too many pastors are dissatisfied with their prayer life. Most Christians long for a dynamic and fruitful prayer life, yet many find themselves defeated when it comes to their communication with God. The same survey indicated that the average church member spends only three to four minutes a day in prayer.

That's not a criticism—just a statement of fact. Conversation with God holds the key to developing intimacy with Him and consistency in our walk with Him. Jesus' life was consistently full of prayer and devotion. Mark 1:35 tells us, "Now in the morning, having risen a long while before daylight, [Jesus] went out and departed to a solitary place; and there He prayed" (NKJV).

And Shaun reminds us that prayer without action gets us nowhere. You need to walk with God. It's a journey, my friends. When we talk and walk with God, He will guide us in the process. A great ship drifting in the sea can't be steered by the captain and crew unless it is moving. And so it is with our lives. No matter our religious upbringing, our works of service, our deep and abiding faith—God can't use us greatly until we engage the throttle of our hearts and shift into a gear that allows Him to direct our paths. The psalmist reminded us that God leads us in the "paths of righteousness" (Psalm 23:3). Spend some time listening to God, and then develop an action plan that moves you into the direction He is taking you. We all need a guide to walk through the maze of challenges, frustrations, confusion, and despair associated with living a productive and positive life.

We were never meant to walk through our lives alone.

No good thing does he withhold
from those whose walk is blameless.
—PSALM 84:11

GAME PLAN:

1. What could you do to develop more time to communicate with God? Could you imagine a place and time that would allow you ten, fifteen, or even twenty minutes a day?

2. What do Genesis 6:9, Psalm 84:11, and Proverbs 10:9 tell you about the importance of walking the walk and having time alone with God?

SEARCHING THROUGH FOOTBALL ANNALS, YOU WILL COME ACROSS NAMES OF THE GREAT COACHES: Amos Alonzo Stagg, Knute Rockne, John Heisman, Paul Brown, Vince Lombardi, George Allen, Weeb Ewbank, Sid Gilman, Bill Walsh, Tom Landry. Some of the greatest coaches today are guys like Tony Dungy, Lovie Smith, and Steve Spagnuolo. These coaches inspire and direct many players to develop fully and utilize their God-given talents to help lead their teams to victory.

Webster's New World Dictionary describes a coach as "the person who is in overall charge of a team and the strategy in games; an instructor or trainer." Today's head coach is more than a good football strategist or educator. He must be a multitalented individual with nerves of steel, the passion of an evangelist, the drive of the apostle Paul, the wisdom of Solomon, the patience of Job, the leadership abilities of a five-star general, the communication skills of a politician, the compassion of a pastor, the applied psychology of a therapist, the persuasion skills of a salesman, and the willingness to work long hours. Most important, he must have a loving, patient family who will support and encourage him through his darkest hours.

What possesses a man to become a head coach? Some evolve into the position because they enjoyed the game as a player and want to continue in the sport. Many coaches started off in high school or college as an assistant. A few came from the ranks of business.

Today, the best coaches seem to be guys who played a limited amount of college or pro ball but who have always desired to lead and direct others to success. They are men who love the game and are full of passion.

A successful coach will surround himself with successful people who share his work ethic, values, philosophy, and fervor for the game. A great coach is an innovator and visionary seeking to add new wrinkles to the game in order to test his opponents' playmaking abilities.

Bill Belichick, Pete Carroll, Jim Harbaugh, Lovie Smith, Mike Shanahan, and Tom Coughlin are coaches who know how to win and continually think outside the box when it comes to play calling. One of the key factors these men share is that of surrounding themselves with smart thinkers and energetic assistant coaches.

From the teachings of the apostle Paul we can assume that he would have made a great football coach. He was fiery and full of passion. Paul surrounded himself with able men who shared his fervor for communicating God's Word. Read his words again and see if you agree: "But one thing I do: Forgetting what is behind and straining toward what is ahead, I press on toward the goal to win the prize for which God has called me heavenward in Christ Jesus" (Philippians 3:13–14). Who do you hang around with? Are they people who support your beliefs and encourage you in your pursuits?

Show me your ways, O LORD, teach me your paths;
guide me in your truth and teach me,
for you are God my Savior,
and my hope is in you all day long.
—PSALM 25:4–5

PRO FOOTBALL IS LIKE NUCLEAR WARFARE.
THERE ARE NO WINNERS—ONLY SURVIVORS.

FRANK GIFFORD

GAME
PLAN:

1. In our leadership roles,
   we are called to be the coach.
   Do your work ethics, values, philosophy, and
   fervor for the game of life encourage others
   to follow your lead?

2. In our worship life, we are called to listen to the
   Coach. Are you a coachable player? Do you seek
   out His will daily in His playbook, the Bible? Ask
   God to create a coachable heart in you each day.

FOOTBALL, LIKE MOST SPORTS, HAS MANY COMPONENTS THAT SEEM PARADOXICAL.

Why is it that the smallest guy on the field is often expected to be the last defense against a raging bull-like running back? Did you ever stop to consider that often players are compensated for what they did in the past and not necessarily how they will perform in the future?

Here's a real paradox: A little rural community in Pine Village, Indiana, was once a national power in the sport of professional football.

In the late 1890s, Clinton Beckett, the principal of the small Pine Village School and a high school teacher, introduced the sport of football to the Villagers. Two teams were formed, one from the high school students and one from former students and twenty-year-olds who then competed for county bragging rights. This tradition continued for almost twenty years.

Some wise entrepreneurs got into the mix and began to buy and sell the rights to utilize some of the former high school players so they could create an independent league. Part-time coaches joined the part-time players on weekends to play a game or two. It is reported that they offered not much more than an opportunity for "drinking and rowdyism." The spectators on the sidelines were more likely to get injured (in a brawl) than the ill-equipped players on the field.

The coaches built a traveling team that began to play some of the other upstart independent teams. Some accounts indicate that the "renegade Pine

Village team was made up of sizable players that played very rough." Newspaper accounts confirm that some teams would refuse to play Pine Village because of their fierce reputation.

For one game the Mickey Athletic Club of Indianapolis came to play Pine Village. They left town almost as quickly as they came after losing by a score of 111–0. This game gave way to more professional contests against teams made up of former college players coached by the famous Knute Rockne and others who took the game much more seriously than Pine Village.

Pine Village played 13 games for the season, scoring 259 points to their opponents' 35 and claiming both the Indiana State Championship and the World Championship. Many of their players were the who's who of football stars from major colleges.

Time passed, and World War I took many able-bodied men away from football to fight America's enemies. By the time the players returned, Pine Village, Indiana, had discovered basketball. Many of the outstanding players were getting too old to play, and it was time to focus on making a living. However, with their history, a small rural community made up of tough twenty-year-olds helped usher in the interest in this new sport that ultimately created the National Football League.

According to Scripture, except for Jesus Christ, King Solomon was the wisest man ever to live. In the book of Ecclesiastes, Solomon pointed out that everything has its time: "To everything there is a season, a time for every purpose under heaven" (3:1 NKJV). And everything, including football, will eventually come to an end, because the end of time is coming.

What are your thoughts regarding the end of this age? Are you ready? Ponder this anonymous message found in an e-mail:

We have taller buildings but shorter tempers; wider freeways but narrower viewpoints; we spend more but have less; we buy more but enjoy it less.

We have bigger houses and smaller families; more conveniences, yet less time; we have more degrees but less sense; more knowledge but less judgment; more experts, yet more problems; more medicine, yet less wellness. . . .

We . . . spend too recklessly; laugh too little; drive too fast; get too angry quickly; stay up too late; get up too tired; read too seldom; watch TV too much and pray too seldom.

We have multiplied our possessions, but reduced our values. . . . We talk too much, love too seldom, and lie too often.

We've learned how to make a living, but not a life; we've added years to life, but not life to years. . . .

We've cleaned up the air, but polluted the soul.

You know very well that the day of the Lord will come like a thief in the night.
—1 THESSALONIANS 5:2

GAME PLAN:

1. There is indeed a time for everything—and God should be in all those times. How can you work to make God and godlike attitudes a part of every moment of your life?

2. We don't know when the end will come, which is why we always need to be prepared. Keep your heart ready for God with daily prayer, Scripture reading, and confession. And then find someone to share Him with.

HEAD FOOTBALL COACH
STANFORD UNIVERSITY
FORMER NFL COACH

« FEATURING »

David Shaw

FAVORITE BIBLE VERSE: PSALM 84:11

For the LORD God is a sun and shield;
the LORD bestows favor and honor;
no good thing does he withhold
from those whose walk is blameless.

I'm often asked the question as to what shaped my coaching style and football philosophy. Certainly watching my dad, Willie Shaw, who had a successful career as a coach impacted my approach to the game. He had the privilege of coaching at five different colleges and with eight NFL teams.

Watching how coaches and players responded to him then, and hearing them talk about the profound influence he had on their careers and lives now, really showed me how much of a positive impact I could make on a young man's life.

I also feel the many lessons I learned while coaching in the NFL under successful head coaches like Brian Billick and Jon Gruden influenced me in forging my own coaching style—having strength and confidence both with a foundation of knowledge, transparent sincerity, and the desire to produce winners on the field, in the classroom, and in life after football.

Since I graduated from Stanford back in 1995, it was a real honor when they selected me to replace Jim Harbaugh as head football coach. The 2011 season tested my character and football philosophy as we became one of the best teams in the NCAA. The nature of my personality is to remain humble while encouraging each player to excel. My passion is to get the best out of each man. I believe it is important that young men trust the judgment of their coaches and recognize the bigger picture of how to be a team player and a good student.

Evangelist F. B. Meyer once said, "The only hope of decreasing self is an increasing of Christ." I have also been deeply influenced by the humility I see in Christ Jesus. He accomplished all He had to do while remaining confident under pressure.

The 2011 season was a unique experience with 21 of my players earning all-conference honors and 5 players, including Andrew Luck, receiving All-American honors. So I may not ever jump in the stands after a game or run up and down the sidelines yelling at officials, but I will continue to work with the knowledge, courage, strength, talents, and faith God has given me to be an encourager.

The apostle Paul probably summed up my thinking best: "Neither do we go beyond our limits by boasting of work done by others. Our hope is that, as your faith continues to grow, our area of activity among you will greatly expand" (2 Corinthians 10:15). Our area of influence will grow as we give credit to others and encourage people with their God-given gifts and talents.

And Jesus grew in wisdom and stature,
and in favor with God and men.
—LUKE 2:52

WHEN AN NFL QUARTERBACK DROPS BACK TO PASS, THE ONE THING HE DOESN'T WANT TO DO IS THROW AN INTERCEPTION. Unfortunately, in the heat of the battle, what a quarterback wants and what can happen to the misguided pigskin may be two different things.

Take the case of quarterback Jim Hardy of the old Chicago Cardinals. On September 24, 1950, against the Philadelphia Eagles, Jim's performance was less than spectacular: he attempted 39 passes and was intercepted a record 8 times in a single game!

Quarterback Brett Favre—who played for the Falcons, Packers, Jets, and Vikings—currently holds the record for most interceptions thrown at over 300. On a more positive note, he also has more than 500 touchdowns to his credit.

Then there are the accurate quarterbacks like Drew Brees, Matt Hasselbeck, Peyton Manning, Eli Manning, and Kurt Warner—precise in their passing and not willing to just chuck the ball into the air and hope for "good things to happen." New England Patriots quarterback Tom Brady still holds the NFL record of attempting 319 passes in a row without a single interception. This was precision at its best.

Today's skilled quarterbacks, operating in the "lower risk" West Coast Offense, often find a better ratio of touchdowns to interceptions. In this offensive scheme, most quarterbacks are attempting high-percentage passes in the 5- to 15-yard range. The 3-step drop and quick release often help them complete throws before the defensive backs have a chance to react.

The possibility of an interception should not deter a quarterback from throwing the ball. An experienced quarterback will make decisions and react accordingly. If the possibility of an interception seems low to moderate, given the possibility for gain, he will throw the ball. Nothing ventured, nothing gained.

One of my favorite quotes on risk-taking comes from the great Teddy Roosevelt: "Far better is it to dare mighty things, to win glorious triumphs even though checkered by failure, than to rank with those poor spirits who neither enjoy nor suffer much because they live in the gray twilight that knows neither victory nor defeat."

To be a successful passer, you need to constantly refine and perfect your skills while taking some risks. The discipline of working on being extremely accurate is of utmost importance. The quarterback's passing drills involve frequent opportunities to "thread the needle" by throwing the pigskin into very tight spots.

So it is with being a disciple of Christ—it's about practice and commitment. Jesus is perpetually involved in perfecting us, the saints, for the work of ministry, and He uses our circumstances in the process. You and I, as disciples, are to make other disciples who can in turn reproduce themselves. Discipleship is apprenticeship—it is the process of sharing, encouraging, modeling, teaching, listening, and serving.

The daily practice of living Christlike lives will help keep us from having our intentions and actions intercepted by the evil one. Be accurate and keep focused!

I DON'T PICK ON
ANYBODY WHO HAS A
NUMBER ABOVE THIRTY.

MIKE DITKA

*"My prayer is not that you take them out of the world
but that you protect them from the evil one."*
—JOHN 17:15

GAME
PLAN:

1. Interceptions by your game-day opponent have costly consequences. But interception by our "life opponent" can have eternal consequences. What can you do today to keep your relationship with God from being intercepted?

2. Read Philippians 4:13. How can this verse help you keep your day from being intercepted?

52 PERSEVERANCE: THE ATHLETE'S FRIEND

WHEN I THINK OF THE PERSEVERANCE NEEDED TO BE A SUCCESSFUL ATHLETE, I'm reminded of my good friend All-Pro Guard Steve Wisniewski, affectionately known as the "Wiz."

Wiz received almost every honor imaginable for his abilities on the gridiron. He appeared in 8 Pro Bowls and was recognized by *Sports Illustrated* as one of the toughest guys in football because of his great strength and perseverance. Amongst his Oakland Raider teammates of the day, Steve was known for his competitive spirit and dynamic power.

After playing the last game of the 1996 season, Wisniewski sat in the locker room and reflected on the difficult year the Raiders had experienced. There were numerous disappointments and lost opportunities that had cost them a chance at the playoffs. He decided to commit himself to becoming an even better athlete and a better person.

He decided to prepare himself for a marathon run. The very next day he met with his strength coach and asked for his help: "Coach, I really want to run a complete marathon. This is something I've got to do!" said the bulky-bodied warrior. His huge frame was not exactly suited for a distance runner. In fact, the coaches were not excited about Steve's decision. They were worried that the tedious running could be detrimental to his knees and back, and they felt the constant pavement pounding necessary to prepare for the long-distance event would ultimately take its toll on their valuable player's body. Linemen are not disciplined to do long-distance running but rather to run with short, powerful bursts of energy.

His first effort at distance was anything but glamorous. He ran a mile and a quarter and collapsed with his lungs burning. "I have never felt so challenged. My big body wasn't made to be tested in that way. I thought I was in good shape until I started jogging for distance," confided the Wiz.

He decided that preparing for a marathon was a good physical and mental discipline to prepare him for life. He had been a Christian since he was a high school athlete, but had never really challenged himself in his faith and personal commitment to serving God. He decided, "Like the apostle Paul I wanted to live a dedicated and committed life. I wanted to dedicate this marathon to God as a personal sacrifice and testimony of my consecrated life" (Hebrews 12:1–29).

He remembered how the perseverance and dedication associated with outdoor sports helped shape his young life. Knowing that an even greater commitment would be required to mold his relationship with God further, he decided that the marathon would serve as a metaphor for the depth of his commitment.

Wiz fixed his gaze on the goal and began a disciplined daily workout that would ultimately lead to participating in the Olympia, Washington, marathon on May 18, 1997. Every day when he hit the track he had one thing in mind: "to honor and glorify God through this testing." Finally, after months of practice, and losing 38 pounds, he lined up with thousands of other runners to begin the 26.2-mile journey to the finish line. Physically, he knew he was in the best condition of his life; the real test would be the mental aspect of the run. [35]

Wiz knew the odds of a man his size finishing a race this long were very slim. While he had prepared himself well, he felt he needed some additional resources to get through the day:

> I decided that I needed some music and some food. I bought a large elastic belt that held my Walkman, extra tapes, and some quick-energy stuff. I hadn't practiced with this equipment and

soon realized that the extra weight and bulk of everything really threw me off. It became an encumbrance to performing the way I had practiced. [36]

After about four miles, he grasped the meaning of Hebrews 12:1: "Therefore, since we are surrounded by such a great cloud of witnesses, let us throw off everything that hinders and the sin that so easily entangles, and let us run with perseverance the race marked out for us."

He ripped off the belt with all its weight and distractions and threw it into a nearby bush, where he could retrieve it later.

It was 5 hours and 33 minutes from the sound of the starting gun when Steve crossed the finish line. He was the last person to finish and one of very few folks over 270 pounds to ever complete a marathon. What he won was a deeper appreciation for the presence of God in his life. He realized the importance of working hard and persevering toward a goal. He recognized that the difference between ordinary and extraordinary is most often a little extra effort. Scripture encourages us to excel and work hard as unto the Lord.

As you know, we consider blessed those who have persevered. You have heard of Job's perseverance and have seen what the Lord finally brought about. The Lord is full of compassion and mercy.

—JAMES 5:11

GAME PLAN:

1. What goal has God put before you?

2. Are you willing to persevere and sacrifice to meet it?

MUCH LIKE THE FRUSTRATIONS OF A LOSING FOOTBALL SEASON, at times life can be full of disappointments. With the advent of salary caps, free agency, and parity, teams that only a few years ago seemed unbeatable can quickly become struggling franchises.

Blame starts popping out and finger-pointing begins as the press, the fans, and the management start to analyze the situation. Within days of a disappointing season, a once successful coaching staff is perhaps at risk of being terminated. Fickle fans start venting their frustrations on talk radio programs as if the host of the show had the power of the team's senior managing partner.

It's interesting to me that a corporate executive can have a bad day at work and life goes on. A stockbroker can choose the wrong investments for his clients and still remain in business. But if a starting coach, quarterback, receiver, or kicker has a bad day, millions will hear about it throughout the week.

As important as football might be to some, the fleeting grief felt from a loss or a bad season may be partially soothed with next week's win or next spring's high draft choice. Most good coaches or players who are let go because of a dismal season will usually find a team willing to give them another try.

Conversely, there are individuals who feel the unrelenting pain of enduring trials: those suffering the challenges associated with fighting a terminal illness, a family abandoned by the mother of the house because she felt she needed a less stressful life, the business associate who had a major financial reversal, or the conscientious pastor who suffers endless slanderous attacks from a few disgruntled parishioners.

There are all kinds of trials and sufferings. Scripture is filled with people

whose great character was molded by the amount of pain and distress they endured. From their stories we are reminded that with suffering comes the opportunity to honor, trust, obey, and know God more intimately. Peter, the longsuffering disciple, reminded us, "After you have suffered for a little while, the God of all grace . . . will Himself perfect, confirm, strengthen and establish you" (1 Peter 5:10 NASB).

While we live out our lives on earth, sufferings can teach us to develop patience and perseverance. I'm thankful that in heaven we won't need to work on these traits; our primary role will be that of praising and worshiping God (Revelation 4–5). We are promised that as we learn to endure today's trials and tribulations, we can expect to receive great rewards in eternity. The greater our earthly challenges, the greater opportunity there will be to glorify God.

We read in Scripture how James and John asked Jesus to let them sit at His right side and at His left side in the kingdom of God. They recognized that eternal rewards would eventually be honored. What they didn't fully grasp was the suffering they would endure to obtain such powerful positions in God's kingdom (Mark 10:35–45).

The Lord wants us to realize that the chief end of every trial is to provide opportunities to:

- gain a greater understanding of God's mercy, kindness, goodness, love, peace, strength, comfort, and goodness;
- further develop our patience, perseverance, and compassion so that our character might be refined;
- comfort others with the love and encouragement we have received;
- obtain the satisfaction and the joy that builds our future capacity to glorify God.

Whether we experience life on a football field or at home, there will be challenges and sufferings. That's life. People who are successful in coping with suffering know that God's grace and love are sufficient to comfort and encourage them through their dilemma. God can use the familiar to teach the incredible. He can turn our nothing into something. We just have to let Him.

If we endure, we will also reign with him.

—2 TIMOTHY 2:12

GAME PLAN:

1. Reflect on a time in your life when you experienced God's faithfulness in the midst of a difficult trial. What did God teach you through that experience?

2. How did that trial deepen your relationship with God?

3. How can you use that experience to help others who may be struggling through a difficult time?

FEW WORDS CAN INTIMIDATE AN NFL QUAR-TERBACK, but one such word is *blitz*. Combine that word with names like 49ers, Patrick Willis, Ravens, Ray Lewis, Packers, Clay Matthews, and Cowboys, De Marcus Warc, and you have the heartbeat of a defense.

The middle linebacker is to a defense what the quarterback is to an offense. He is the playmaker, the one everyone looks to for guidance, inspi-ration, and advice. He is the coach's eyes and ears on defense.

The linebacker must be one of the most gifted athletes on the field. Whatever the offensive or defensive scheme, he must provide a triple threat. He must be quick enough to cover a running back on a short pass route, he must rush the passer while fending off the blocks of the big offensive line-men, and he must be able to stack up a running play that may take him from sideline to sideline.

A good linebacker knows that every offensive alignment brings a certain strength and weakness. Depending on the defensive formation, they can either overplay the opponent's strength or prey upon their weakness.

Someone once said, "Pain is something that separates linebackers from everyone else on the field—both dishing it out and receiving it."

Former Bears coach Mike Ditka was a real believer in tough linebackers. He once asked Mike Singletary, "When's the last time you broke a helmet?" When Singletary replied that it had been awhile, Ditka challenged him, "I want to hear one break." While playing at Baylor University, Singletary broke sixteen helmets, all of them his own. [37]

IMMEDIATELY AFTER KURT WARNER AND THE RAMS' VICTORY IN SUPER BOWL XXXIII, AN INTERVIEWER SAID, "KURT, FIRST THINGS FIRST— TELL ME ABOUT THE TOUCHDOWN PASS TO IASAAC [BRUCE]." WARNER RESPONDED, "WELL, FIRST THINGS FIRST, I'VE GOT TO THANK MY LORD AND SAVIOR UP ABOVE— THANK YOU, JESUS!"

KURT WARNER,
Super Bowl XXXIII MVP

At times Christians are called upon to play tough. When it comes to dealing with sin that could impact our loved ones or ourselves, God wants us to knock it down before it gets started. A linebacker's training and discipline is such that the battle on the field becomes natural—he tries to anticipate and prepares himself for the hit. So it is with a Christian. We must immerse ourselves in God's Word and train ourselves in His ways so that our reaction to sin becomes intuitive. Preparation is the key.

If anybody does sin, we have one who speaks to the Father in our defense—Jesus Christ, the Righteous One.
—1 JOHN 2:1

GAME PLAN:

1. Are you fending off the attacks of the enemy, or is he taking advantage of your weaknesses?

2. What do you need to do to prepare for attacks from the Enemy in order to mount an effective defense?

LONG BEFORE I ARRIVED IN THIS WORLD, A TALL BUT SLENDER MAN NAMED DON HUTSON JOINED THE GREEN BAY PACKERS. Hutson was from the University of Alabama, where he had been an All-American on his senior team, a Rose Bowl winner. His patented catching style eventually placed him in the NFL Hall of Fame.

For eleven seasons, Hutson set records that still exist today. Years after he retired his legacy still prevailed. Talk of his precise routes and game-winning catches still lingered in locker-room conversations among defensive players. After looking at some old game footage and hearing current commentators who are still talking about Hutson, you realize he had moves that even the best receivers have difficulty emulating. He'd catch the ball and twist away from a guy going to tackle him in a split second. If you see enough of his moves, you begin to wonder if he was a contortionist, ghost, or magician.

It was Hutson, not the great wide receivers of today, who elevated receiving into an art form. Don Hutson still holds several NFL records and is considered the ultimate precision-pattern receiver.

Not only was Hutson agile and cunning, but he also had drive and passion to catch the ball—so much so that he became known for the concentrated moment of catching a pass as "looking the ball into your hands." Hutson's size was no factor in how or where he caught the ball. He didn't shy away from crossing over the middle and taking a lick from an angry safety or middle linebacker. Mark Twain once said, "It's not the size of the dog in a fight, but the size of the fight in the dog"—and that was certainly true about Hutson. Don had a mission and a motivation to be the very best . . . and he was.

As we have seen, being a great football player requires enormous effort, focus, passion, and commitment, as well as an inward strength of character. This internal power comes first from recognizing our deficits and short-comings.

Being a dedicated follower of Jesus also requires tremendous strength of character and a relationship with God that is built first upon acknowledging our inner weaknesses. The apostle Paul said, "If I must boast, I will boast of the things that show my weakness . . . so that Christ's power may rest on me" (2 Corinthians 11:30; 12:9).

As with Paul's thorn in the flesh, our defects are continual reminders of our need for a caring, loving, compassionate, merciful, gracious Savior. Some say that men are tough; they can handle their problems. But true strength comes through admitting our inadequacies. It is when we acknowledge our true dependence on our Creator that we can really find the ultimate strength and power that separates us from the sins and problems of the world. Paul underscored this concept: "I can do all things through Christ who strengthens me" (Philippians 4:13 NKJV).

Whom have I in heaven but you?
And earth has nothing I desire besides you.
My flesh and my heart may fail,
but God is the strength of my heart
and my portion forever.
—PSALM 73:25–26

SELF-PRAISE IS FOR LOSERS.
BE A WINNER. STAND FOR SOMETHING.
ALWAYS HAVE CLASS, AND BE HUMBLE.

JOHN MADDEN

GAME
PLAN:

1. As you go to God in prayer today, confess to Him your weakness and ask that He strengthen you with His power.

2. Rejoice in the fact that even though you may struggle here on earth, eternal joy and peace await you as a child of God.

ANYONE EVEN CASUALLY ACQUAINTED WITH PROFESSIONAL FOOTBALL IS AWARE OF HOW THE VARIOUS FANS CELEBRATE A SCORE. Some have special chants, cheers, or even choreographed routines to express their joy in their team.

And for every celebration by one team, there is equal disappointment demonstrated by the opposing team. The lists of potential excuses are many: someone called the wrong alignment, a critical block or tackle was missed, or maybe a defensive player was simply physically mismatched with his opponent. The reactions of fans can be downright caustic. Equally embarrassing can be the way players respond to the problem. Some will hang their heads and walk dejectedly off the field. Others might literally point the fickle finger of blame at someone else. Sometimes players run off the field to yell at a coach or another player.

Most recently, it has been the custom of embarrassed athletes to literally point the finger of blame at themselves. It is as if they purposely move into an open area of the field and begin head-nodding while pounding their chest as if to say, "It's me! I'm the one to blame!"

For a Christian, confession is the first step toward defeating the issue of blame or, in this case, sin. Sometimes the hardest part of dealing with a problem is admitting that you have one. People naturally want to deny responsibility for their failings. Some wish to blame their behavior on bad parenting, the culture in which they were raised, the lack of a proper education, or even that somehow God is against them.

THERE ARE A THOUSAND
REASONS FOR FAILURE
BUT NOT A SINGLE EXCUSE.

MIKE REID,
Former Bengal Lineman

Confession, though, is simply agreeing with God about our sin. It affirms our dependence on a forgiving, merciful Lord who can deal with our failures in a righteous way. By confessing, we restore God's blessing upon our lives.

God's people have always recognized the importance of confession. David acknowledged to Nathan the prophet, and then to God, "I have sinned against the LORD" (2 Samuel 12:13 NASB). As we saw earlier, when Isaiah saw the holiness of God in a vision he declared, "Woe is me, for I am ruined! Because I am a man of unclean lips, and I live among a people of unclean lips" (Isaiah 6:5 NASB). Even Daniel, who had tremendous integrity, confessed his sin: "I was speaking and praying, confessing my sin and the sin of my people Israel and making my request to the LORD my God for his holy hill" (Daniel 9:20).

Ongoing confession of sin to God distinguishes a mature believer. Those who claim to be believers but refuse to confess their sins deceive themselves (1 John 1:8) and make God a liar (1 John 1:10). Next time you feel like pointing at someone else about a problem, make sure you first consider what sin exists in your own life. As Jesus reminded us, "Why do you look at the speck of sawdust in your brother's eye and pay no attention to the plank in your own eye?" (Matthew 7:3).

GAME PLAN:

1. Read 1 John 1:8–2:6. This passage of Scripture is a great reminder that it is only through Jesus and His sacrifice that God views us as clean. Without Christ—without the atoning sacrifice that He made for us—we'd be doomed!

2. Take time to examine your relationship with God. Where are you failing? What can you do to improve and deepen your walk with God?

« FEATURING »

David Akers

FAVORITE BIBLE VERSE: ROMANS 5:3–5

We also rejoice in our sufferings, because we know that suffering produces perseverance; perseverance, character; and character, hope. And hope does not disappoint us, because God has poured out his love into our hearts by the Holy Spirit, whom he has given us.

Most people review my life focus on my football achievements. I can't deny that it was a great honor being named to the NFL All-Decade Team in 2010 and playing six times in the Pro Bowl. Considering that three teams initially cut me because of my sporadic performance, I believe my successes were a product of hard work, perseverance, and the grace of God.

I think the most exciting year in football came during my 2011 season with the 49ers. As a kicker, I was privileged to be on a team that often had difficulty punching the ball into the end zone; hence, I was frequently called upon to kick some field goals. I was blessed to make 44 out of 52 attempts and even throw a touchdown pass on a trick play. Who would have thought that, at 37 years old, I would rack up 166 points and set a new league record for kickers? I was told that I even passed the great Jerry Rice for the most points in one season. I was equally honored when Coach Jim Harbaugh named me as the "most valuable player and one of the team's best leaders" for the 2011–2012 season. Then on September 9, 2012, while playing the Greenbay Packers, I had the opportunity to kick the longest field goal in NFL history and tie the record with Jason Elam, Sebastian Janikowski, and Tom Dempsey, who also kicked 63 yard field goals.

It's amazing to think that only a year before my time with the 49ers my world was falling apart. After being swindled out of most of my savings and cut from the Eagles after missing 2 field goals in a playoff game, I didn't think life could get any worse. Then the news came that my beautiful 6-year-old daughter, Halley, was diagnosed with an ovarian tumor. As important as football was to my life and legacy, I would have given it all up for the two most important things in my life—faith and family.

In the past, I had regularly raised money and visited many patients at the Children's Hospital of Philadelphia with my Kick for Kids program. I would always come home from visiting the cancer floors and hug my kids and thank God that they were healthy. It was a real paradox when my wife, Erika, and I arrived at the same hospital seeking a miracle treatment for our little girl.

It was during Halley's trials that our faith in God was tested. It was then our family cherished the words of encouragement found in Scripture. I especially connected with the apostle Paul and his many struggles. Paul's life is a testimony of the suffering servant. For anyone facing the struggles life brings, even a parent's worst nightmare, Paul told us to hang in there. God is at work building our faith and character.

DURING THE 1950S AND 1960S, THERE WAS ONE NAME THAT BECAME SYNONYMOUS WITH FOOTBALL—JOHNNY UNITAS. During these great growth years of the NFL, Unitas helped carry the sport to the forefront. His work ethic and passion for the game provided his teammates with great inspiration.

Unitas was a self-made man of sorts. His father died early in his life, leaving his family in a desperate situation. Johnny observed his mother's hard work as she returned to night school to further her education while scrubbing floors during the day to make enough money to feed her family.

To help out, the young Unitas shoveled two tons of coal every day after school to help his mom provide for the family. Somehow he squeezed in enough practice time to play varsity football. As hard as he played, no major college was interested in a 5'11", 130-pound quarterback. When hope seemed gone, Unitas began to promote his talents to a few colleges. Notre Dame was probably more worried about Johnny being hurt than if he could lead the Irish to a championship.

Finally Unitas got a break when the University of Louisville took a chance on him. His college football successes won him a ninth-round draft pick from the Pittsburgh Steelers. Unfortunately, he was cut in his rookie year prior to the beginning of the season. However, rather than quit football, Unitas decided to keep his skills sharp by playing semi-pro ball at $6 a game. In the "rock 'em, sock 'em" league, he once again proved his skill and passion while playing for the Bloomfield Rams.

Finally, the Colts phoned Unitas and asked him to try out at their May camp. Unitas made the Colts as a backup quarterback. When the starting quarterback went down with a leg injury, Johnny was inserted into the game.

His inexperience was obvious. He fumbled 3 times and his first throw was greeted with an interception. But failure was something Unitas didn't accept.

While many coaches would have scolded him, the team decided to go with Johnny as their quarterback. Unitas went on to become one of the most successful players in NFL history.

Unitas wrote the playbook on what it takes to win a game in the last 2 minutes. His style was a mixture of pure genius and pure recklessness. He would run down the field ahead of his runners, blocking anyone in his way. Despite his stature he seemed to adopt the philosophy, "If you show fear, you've already lost the game."

Not only did he appear in 10 Pro Bowls and win 3 league MVP awards, but he also called most of the offensive plays from the huddle during 1958–1971. He masterminded the overtime comeback of the Baltimore Colts in what is arguably the greatest game ever played—the 1958 NFL Championship game with the New York Giants. He also threw at least 1 touchdown pass in each of 47 consecutive games, a record that stood until October of 2012, when Drew Brees with the New Orleans Saints broke it.

His blue-collar image endeared him to the common laborer. His high-top boots and in-your-face play gave him enormous crowd appeal. One commentator said this about the legendary man: "When the image of the best player to play the game matches the substance—that is Johnny Unitas."

The image of Johnny Unitas is a picture of a determined warrior. His matchless willpower and desire for success helped him become one of the top players to ever lace up a pair of football cleats. Winston Churchill said of those who are determined, "Some people dream of success, while others wake up and work hard at it."

Unitas mirrors the determination found in several biblical characters. One such person is a young, undersized lad named David. David was not seen to have warrior potential. He was slight of build and seemed to be suited more for watching sheep than slaying the enemy.

And much like the character and determination we see in Johnny U., David worked hard to sell himself to others. He finally convinced his brothers and King Saul to let him have a chance to prove himself and his Lord. With God's help, David took on a very tough assignment. The Spirit of God directed his every move as he flung a small rock to triumph over the monstrous Philistine, Goliath.

David was confident and determined because he knew that with God's help anything is possible. We serve a God who regularly deals with impossible situations. He is the Lord of all possibilities. So it is, my friends: Persevere! Be determined! If a scrawny young boy from a small coal mining town can become one of the NFL's most distinguished quarterbacks, and if a frail shepherd boy can slay a giant, God can enable you to do far more than you might expect.

For God did not give us a spirit of timidity,
but a spirit of power, of love and of self-discipline.
—2 TIMOTHY 1:7

GAME PLAN:

1. How does God's standard of success differ from the world's?

2. Like David, how are you allowing God to build you into a successful person?

SOME TIME AGO DEION SANDERS, AKA "NEON DEION" OR "PRIME TIME," STATED, "As a kid I admired many athletes for certain traits they displayed . . . and incorporated them into myself." He liked the brashness and confidence of Muhammad Ali; he also emulated the focus Hank Aaron had during his chase of Babe Ruth's home-run record. Similarly, Prime Time liked the class and respect demonstrated by Julius Erving on and off the basketball court.

However, Sanders was quick to remind us, "These weren't the people who ultimately instilled my morals and taught me right from wrong." He places that responsibility with his parents and on a pastor friend, Bishop T. D. Jakes. "Kids put athletes on pedestals a little too much," said Sanders. "We really are just human." He went on to say, "Some of the greatest role models are found at home or in our churches." [38]

Prime Time had his days of scoring touchdowns and dancing in the end zone. But after the stadium full of cheering fans had gone home, he was empty inside. His pursuit of power, money, and sex had not produced its perceived happiness. There was a void that no amount of adoration could fill. It's a long way from 80,000 people screaming your name to one person telling you to take out the trash.

His view of success changed with his commitment to follow Jesus. Deion realized that pursuing integrity and character were second only to seeking a personal relationship with God. He devoted himself to becoming a new man—a man after God's own heart and a person of great integrity.

NEVER LET HOPE ELUDE YOU.
THAT IS LIFE'S BIGGEST FUMBLE.

BOB ZUPPKE

In a similar manner, the Babylonian captivity of the Jews set the stage for more than one truly uncommon display of integrity and character from Daniel and his three friends. First, Shadrach, Meshach, and Abednego refused to bow down to the king's idol—at great risk to their own lives (Daniel 3). Later, Daniel risked death by refusing to pray to the king (Daniel 6). These men could have hidden their faith, but instead they showed great strength of character by refusing to do so. God can use such strength of character to strengthen not only His people but also to show the world His power and faithfulness.

> He holds victory in store for the upright,
> he is a shield to those whose walk is blameless,
> for he guards the course of the just
> and protects the way of his faithful ones.
> —PROVERBS 2:7–8

GAME PLAN:

1. Are there people in your life you try to emulate in some way? Are their characteristics in line with how Jesus would want you to be and act?

2. Think of a time you had the opportunity to show your integrity and character by standing up for God. How did it impact your life and those around you?

IN FOOTBALL, EACH PLAYER TOILS AT HIS JOB, HOPING TO WIN HIS INDIVIDUAL BATTLES. Each player brings his own dynamic to the game: for some it's about intimidation; for others it's a quiet but powerful exercise of God-given abilities; with a few players the battle is won through analysis and applied wisdom. There are times when it seems the energy and tension on the field is almost palpable. The totals on the scoreboard can at times be overshadowed by the personal battles on the field.

The spectators also provide entertainment. Some, filled with exuberance, voice their approval or disapproval with deafening yells or shouts of joy. Others sit calmly waving their team's banner. And we can't overlook those spectators who get so involved in the game they actually dress up in costume, making sure to spread an ample supply of war paint on any exposed flesh. This prepares them for their role in winning the game.

The Christian experience is a great deal like the game of football. While the battle between good and evil is waging within families, in the workplace, and in the hearts of those who don't yet know the love, peace, and comfort God can provide, many Christians sit by calmly, watching events unfold. Until you become personally engaged in the struggles life brings, or make yourself available to help others who are hurting, you can't really appreciate pain.

Unfortunately, too many Christians find themselves merely spectators of life. They assume that full-time pastors and missionaries are the only ones charged with the responsibilities of ministering to others. The tragedy of September 11, 2001, in New York; Washington, DC; and Pennsylvania woke people up to the fact that as a nation, or as a community, or as a family, we need to get involved in helping others.

Throughout the New Testament, we read of God's desire for each person to fully utilize his gifts and talents to serve others. When we bury our treasured abilities, we make a grave mistake. Such was the case with an old violin collector named Luigi Tarisio, who took great pride in searching out and purchasing rare and unusual instruments. Yet, some of his greatest treasures were hidden away. After his death, when his home was inspected and the attic opened to appraise his estate, no fewer than 24 Stradivarius violins were found, along with 120 other Italian violins.

One of the most expensive violins was hidden in an old piece of furniture. It was a rare Stradivarius that probably had not been played in over a hundred years. The grand instrument had gone un-played for over a century. Tarisio had selfishly robbed the world of its beautiful music. [39]

God has given each of us unique spiritual gifts, aptitudes, abilities, and talents (read 1 Corinthians 12 and Romans 12). No two people are the same. What you might think is a common talent may in fact be a uniquely shaped personal trait that can be of real encouragement to others. We can rob ourselves as well as others of a wonder-filled life by hiding our gifts in a "humble" personality. God expects us to refine and perfect our gifts through practice and participation rather than simply being a spectator. He wants us to share our talents.

Just as a football game can stimulate a crowd of fans to a happy experience, so can you bring joy and encouragement to others as you use your God-given treasures. What is your spiritual gift (hospitality, giving, teaching, mercy, exhortation, discernment, wisdom)? In 2 Timothy 1:6, we are encouraged to "fan into flame the gift of God" as we develop our abilities. Let's not become so earthly minded that we fail to use the gifts designed with eternal value. Get in the game!

SETTING A GOAL IS NOT THE MAIN THING.
IT IS DECIDING HOW YOU WILL GO ABOUT
ACHIEVING IT AND STAYING WITH THAT PLAN.

TOM LANDRY

GAME
 PLAN:

1. Are you in the game for God,
   or are you watching from the
   sidelines?

2. How has God uniquely gifted you to
   serve Him as well as others?

3. What are you doing to refine—and
   use—the talents that God has given you?

MOST PEOPLE WOULD DEFINE COURAGE AS BEING FEARLESS, HAVING A DARING SPIRIT THAT ENABLES YOU TO MEET INTIMIDATING CHALLENGES HEAD ON, having true grit. The word *courage* actually comes from the French word *coeur*, which means "heart." Just as the heart lies at the body's core, enabling other parts of the body to function, so courage is central to the Christian, empowering us to manifest other qualities of Christlike character.

To play effectively as a tight end in professional football and to be selected numerous times to represent your conference in the Pro Bowl, you must have courage. To be named as a member of John Madden's "Tough Guy" team, you must be worthy of that title. These are among the highest honors given in the NFL—and both were attained by Brent Jones, former tight end of the San Francisco 49ers.

The 49ers started the 1996 season a little slow, as did Jones. He'd had only four passes directed to him, and the offense was looking pretty lethargic. After a loss to Carolina, the 49ers vowed to turn things around, but as they prepared for the Atlanta game, disaster struck. The sports section headline in the Saturday paper conveyed the bad news: "Jones to Have Shoulder Surgery." The article read:

> The 49er tight end jinx has struck again. . . . Brent Jones is scheduled for arthroscopic surgery this afternoon to remove an old screw that came loose in his shoulder. . . . Jones partially dislocated his left shoulder in a contact scrimmage Thursday when teammates fell on him. [40]

This was not Jones's first time to be seriously injured. The shoulder had originally been repaired after a separation in high school. Then Jones was in a serious automobile accident, which damaged his neck. In 1995, he was hit hard, and his knee collapsed; he had to be carried off the field only to return a few plays later. Time and time again coaches, reporters, and doctors counted him down and out—finished. Each time God provided a miracle, and Jones displayed the courage that allowed him to return with more passion and persistence than he had before.

Jones went back to his position, making remarkable catches and runs. The 49ers marched on to yet another playoff berth. Fans remember that season with a sense of awe at the determination and courage this man modeled in his life.

However, the biggest battle was off the field. While desire, courage, and guts are admirable qualities in an All-American football player, they can stand in the way of a deep spiritual life. Jones realized that he could only be successful if he placed Jesus Christ at the center of his universe.

God needed to be in control—not Brent! He said, "When I sought to do things on my strength, I usually failed. Things would really get out of whack when I tried to rely on my own wisdom and efforts. When I finally accepted Jesus as my personal Savior and Lord, that's when things really got under control. Proverbs 3:5–6 is real clear on where I need to be with the issue of control: 'Trust in the LORD with all your heart and lean not on your own understanding; in all your ways acknowledge him, and he will make your paths straight.'"

Someone once said, "Courage is not the absence of fear, but the conquest of it." There are at least two types of courage. First, there is the attitude or ability to deal with anything recognized as dangerous, difficult, or painful, instead of running from it. Next is having the boldness to do what one thinks is right. Both definitions fit the profile of Brent Jones.

Like King David, Brent calls upon "the name of the LORD Almighty" (1 Samuel 17:45) to be with him in battles on the line of scrimmage. Because of Jones's physical limitations after his injuries, everyone knows that the glory will go to the Lord.

When you have been protected, encouraged, and strengthened for battle, where does the glory go? Like Brent Jones, do you declare, "The LORD is the strength of my life; of whom shall I be afraid?" (Psalm 27:1 NKJV).

You say, "But, Jim, I *am* afraid!" Eddie Rickenbacker, who regularly pushed the envelope of discovery and exploration, said, "Courage is doing what you're afraid to do. There can be no courage unless you're scared."

Every time you approach a new challenge, look to God for the strength and power. Seek His counsel and move forward with courage. You will gain new strength and assurance each time you experience intimidating situations, approach fear head on, stare it down, and do the thing you think you can't. If it is of God, He will provide a way when there seems to be none.

Whether you're an All-Pro football player or a couch-bound fan, your calling is a courageous one—to be a disciple of the living Christ.

The LORD is my strength and my song;
he has become my salvation.
He is my God, and I will praise him.
—EXODUS 15:2

GAME PLAN:

1. What is your answer to the question above: When you have been protected, encouraged, and strengthened for battle, where does the glory go?

2. How can you better rely on God for the strength and power necessary to battle the challenges of life?

COACHES WORK HARD WITH PLAYERS TO DEVELOP IN THEM THE SKILLS NEEDED TO PROTECT THE BALL AT ALL COSTS. Most NFL teams conduct a regular drill in which the runner scampers past a group of heavy-handed linemen who attempt to knock the ball away.

Fumbles, failures, goofs—whatever you call them—do strange things to a team's confidence. They can be momentum breakers and can produce lost games—both in sports and in life. On the flip side, however, when too much attention is placed upon these occasional failures, it can cost a good player his confidence and his composure.

What do Michael Vick, Robert Griffin III, Cam Newton, Matt Cassel, Mark Sanchez, and Phillip Rivers have in common? Yes, they are all NFL quarterbacks, and after only 5 games into the 2012 season they all have had 5 or more fumbles. Michael Vick had 8 fumbles in this period of time. It is curious that quarterbacks, whom we think of as having gifted hands, have lost the ball more than running backs.

How often have you dropped the ball? Maybe you missed a critical appointment at work. Or perhaps you forgot your child's or even your spouse's birthday. If we place too much attention on our missed opportunities, we can become ineffective and depressed.

Despite our shortcomings, God can use each of us to build His kingdom. I think too many people feel unworthy because they place too much focus upon their failures instead of on the graciousness of a loving God.

Too often we glorify Bible characters and believe that our ability to serve God is less than those "saintly" prophets and apostles of yesterday. It is encouraging to remember that our heavenly Father has equipped each one of us with special talents. He wants us to utilize these gifts rather than be overly critical of our failures. Think about how God used biblical characters despite their imperfections:

- Moses stuttered.
- David's armor didn't fit.
- John Mark was rejected by Paul.
- Hosea's wife was a prostitute.
- Amos's only training was in the school of fig tree pruning.
- Solomon was too rich.
- Abraham was too old.
- Did I mention that Moses had a short fuse? So did Peter, Paul—well, lots of folks did.

Aren't we glad God doesn't keep an account of our fumbles? He is quick to forgive and forget; despite a bad year He still has us in His lineup next season. He doesn't require a job interview. He doesn't hire and fire like human bosses, because He's more than just a boss. He's not prejudiced or partial, not judging, grudging, sassy, or brassy, not deaf to our cry or blind to our need. He knows how we are formed. He remembers we are dust (Psalm 103:14).

If we are totally in love with Him, if we hunger for Him more than for our next breath, He'll use us in spite of who we are, where we've been, or what we look like. Step out of your limitations and into the illimitable nature of who God is.

It was he who gave some to be apostles, some to be prophets, some to be evangelists, and some to be pastors and teachers, to prepare God's people for works of service, so that the body of Christ may be built up until we all reach unity in the faith and in the knowledge of the Son of God and become mature, attaining to the whole measure of the fullness of Christ.

—EPHESIANS 4:11–13

GAME PLAN:

1. Do you believe that God is able to use you in spite of your failures and shortcomings?

2. Are you willing to let Him use you through your failures and shortcomings?

LEADERSHIP IS THE POWER TO EVOKE THE PROPER RESPONSE FROM OTHERS IN ORDER TO OBTAIN A SELECTED GOAL. People who have good leadership skills are usually those who have been tested and tried under stressful situations. Walter Lippmann said, "The final test of a leader is that he leaves behind him in other men the conviction and the will to carry on."

The fall and winter are times when every weekend and Monday night we see outstanding examples of young men displaying leadership skills that can help encourage and motivate their football teams to victory. We call them warriors of the gridiron.

When surveying players and coaches as to what makes a good team leader, words like *dedication*, *commitment*, *passion*, *perseverance*, *determination*, and *mental toughness* come up. As we closely observe marquee players and see the way others look up to them, we are impressed that they model these qualities in every aspect of their lives. These traits become second nature to them.

Over the past twenty years, I've observed many talented coaches and players. It's interesting to see vibrant leadership traits emerge during stressful situations. Let's look at just a few of the qualities good leaders possess:

- They are quick to encourage others.
- They recognize the value and importance of promoting and utilizing the gifts of others to accomplish a goal.

- Leaders will direct people to a positive future and vision.

- Influential people will motivate others to achieve their very best.

- They will strive to maintain unity and harmony among their teammates.

- Naturally gifted people will take charge and earn respect by modeling a proper attitude and exemplary behavior.

- Great leaders sacrifice for others so that their common vision might be reached.

I'm reminded of a story about certain sailors in ancient times who displayed unbelievable leadership. During the time of Christ, the strongest swimmer in a ship's crew was called *archegos*, a Greek word that means "chief leader" or "pioneer." When a ship approached an unstable shoreline, where a safe beach landing was not assured, captains would call upon the *archegos* to jump into the pounding surf and swim ashore with a rope fastened to his waist. Once ashore he would fasten the long rope from the boat to the landing, usually seeking out a large rock or significant tree to quickly secure the line. Then the other passengers and crew could disembark and use the rope as a safety tether to reach the shore.

As Christians, Jesus is our *archegos*. He has gone before us to secure our way home. Without His sacrificial death and resurrection we would be lost—our individual Christian lives would be a frustrating exercise in futility. As the apostle Paul stated, "If we have hoped in Christ in this life only [meaning, if Christ has not been resurrected], we are of all men most to be pitied" (1 Corinthians 15:19 NASB). But Jesus left us with a brighter hope: "For the wages of sin is death, but the free gift of God is eternal life in Christ Jesus our Lord" (Romans 6:23).

Likewise, if all there is to life is the next NFL game, we above all men are to be pitied.

FOOTBALL IS A GAME PLAYED WITH ARMS,
LEGS, AND SHOULDERS,
BUT MOSTLY FROM THE NECK UP.

KNUTE ROCKNE

GAME PLAN:

1. Pray for the ability to develop the leadership skills needed to be an *archegos* for your family, friends, church, and community.

2. Think of someone in particular who is lacking Christ in his or her life. How can you be an *archegos* to that person?

TENNESSEE TITANS
THREE-TIME PRO BOWL
QUARTERBACK IN SUPER BOWL XL
GREEN BAY PACKERS,
SEATTLE SEAHAWKS,
TENNESSEE TITANS

« FEATURING »

Matt Hasselbeck

FAVORITE BIBLE VERSE: COLOSSIANS 3:23

*Whatever you do, work at it with all your heart,
as working for the Lord, not for men.*

I used to dream about legends like Hall of Famers Steve Young, Troy Aikman, Sonny Jurgensen, and Y. A. Tittle, and even tried to emulate them in my style of play and commitment to football excellence. It never occurred to me that I would end up passing for more yards than these great men. At the close of the 2011 season, my 33,150 passing yards inched me past these icons of the NFL.

As I pondered the record books and saw that I was ranked 24th on the all-time quarterback chart, I had to reflect upon the outstanding parenting and coaching I received during my growing-up years. From an early age my Christian parents instilled in me the importance of faith and family before sports activities.

I wanted the joy of my faith to become my mantra like it was for former teammates Reggie White and Trent Dilfer. While they were excellent in their jobs, they were devoted and passionate about their faith. From these guys and my study of God's Word, I found three metaphors from football that helped me disciple others:

1. **If a receiver isn't open, don't force the play—check down to other receivers. Jesus teaches us to be humble, authentic, and transparent about our faith, but if people aren't receptive, then try others.** "If anyone will not welcome you or listen to your words, shake the dust off your feet when you leave that home or town" (Matthew 10:14).

2. **Football is a team sport. I can't be successful on my own. In a similar manner—life cannot be played alone. We need the encouragement and support of others.** "Therefore encourage one another and build each other up, just as in fact you are doing" (1 Thessalonians 5:11).

3. **Whether on or off the field, be a man of integrity. More important than fame or fortune, power or success, is our character.** "Judge me, O LORD, according to my righteousness, according to my integrity, O Most High" (Psalm 7:8).

At the end of the day, where I place in the record books as an All-Pro quarterback isn't as important as my faith, family, and character which have led me to excel as a football player and man of God.

And we know that in all things God works for the good of those who love him, who have been called according to his purpose.

—ROMANS 8:28

IN THE SUMMER OF 2001 PLAYERS SWARMED TO VARIOUS FOOTBALL TRAINING CAMP FACILITIES ACROSS THE NATION, expecting the same old thing. Anticipation ran high as they became accustomed to the two-a-day drills associated with preparing for a rigorous season. No one expected 2001 to be defined by numerous peculiar occurrences that would impact every player's future.

In the middle of the year, one began to wonder if this strange NFL season could become any more bizarre before experiencing the final game, the Super Bowl, slated for February instead of January. Some of the unusual events included:

- A player dies during training camp from heat stroke.

- A few players are suspended for the season because of drug use.

- A game is canceled just minutes before kickoff in front of a national television audience, and a city is embarrassed because their artificial turf was not ready for play.

- College officials replaced striking NFL referees for the first few regular season games.

- A group of fans sue a team over season tickets.

- More rookie quarterbacks take starting jobs than in any other season.

- Thirteen teams start new quarterbacks.

- The All-Pro quarterback who led his team to a Super Bowl victory the previous season was released and is playing for another team.

- The season was put on hold for ten days while our nation grieved the loss of thousands of victims associated with the terrorist attacks.

- New security policies and policing of what can be taken to a game are strictly enforced.

- NFL team training and office facilities are placed under armed security.

- In the last week of regular play eight teams still have a shot to lock up a playoff berth.

- Fans actually appreciate and sing the national anthem at games.

Change is inevitable! There are times in our lives and in the course of a season that demand drastic alterations be made so that we can adapt to the situation.

The world around us is perpetually changing. Values and character are constantly being challenged. What we blushed at only a few years ago is now seen as common language and action. Those unmentionables are now freely discussed on television and radio talk shows. Like the pendulum on a grandfather clock, social standards vacillate back and forth.

With all the change going on in the world, it's good to know that there are some things that will never change—like our Lord. As believers we can count on it: "I the LORD do not change. So you, O descendants of Jacob, are not destroyed" (Malachi 3:6).

The most together players I know—on the football field and in the game of life—recognize this unchanging nature of God and seek the stability in life that can only come through a personal relationship with Him.

HURT IS IN THE MIND. YOU'VE GOT TO MAKE YOURSELF TOUGH AND YOU'VE GOT TO PLAY WHEN IT HURTS. THAT'S WHEN YOU PLAY BEST, WHEN IT HURTS. IF YOU DON'T WANT TO GET HURT, THEN DON'T PLAY FOOTBALL.

HARRY LOMBARDI,
to his son Vince when he broke his leg playing football

Jesus Christ is the same yesterday and today and forever.
—HEBREWS 13:8

GAME PLAN:

1. In the midst of this constantly changing world, with all its trials, struggles, and temptations, do you immediately cling to God as your solid, unmovable foundation?

2. To keep ourselves from being pulled off course, it's important to connect with God through His Word and through prayer on a consistent basis. Make sure you do that today—and every day.

64. FOOTBALL AND HOPE

NEXT TO NASCAR, FOOTBALL RANKS AS THE TOP SPECTATOR SPORT IN THE UNITED STATES. Fans will often debate about whether college football is more exciting than the NFL, or whether arena football is a real game. After all the arguing settles down, we find a slight difference in rules, size of the fields, or the continued rivalry between the AFC and the NFC. But mere tongue exercises do not take away from the unique excitement this sport brings to our culture. Fans experience something vicariously when they watch big, quick, talented men work to a point of near exhaustion in order to move a little air-filled bag of leather up and down a field, mostly oblivious to the pain they are administering to others.

The original rugby/soccer-styled game, later called football, has grown dramatically in its popularity from the early 1890s. Amos Alonzo Stagg, Pop Warner, and other pioneers would probably not recognize today's game. Put the word *football* into your Internet search engine, and you'll find hundreds of supportive sites dealing with topics from "Women in Football" to "God and Football."

Twenty-four hours a day, radio and TV sports talk stations beam their messages of hope and doom to all who wish to listen. There are speculators, prophets, reporters, bookies, and stockholders—all of whom consider themselves experts.

Still, with all its adulation and pomp, football is football. It is played one down at a time; often gains are measured one yard at a time. With all the innovation and new technology, the most constant standard found in any huddle, on any bench, and in any locker room remains as it was from the beginning—hope!

A player enters training camp with the *hope* of making the team. Then he must *hope* that his skills and knowledge so impress the coaches that he will be selected to be a starter. Once the game starts, the player *hopes* he can remember all his assignments. Then he *hopes* his physical and emotional capabilities are up to the challenges and stresses he will face week after week. With each tackle there is the *hope* that he won't sustain a career-ending injury; even top players are only one play away from retirement.

The *hope*-filled life of a player continues as he expects to make it to the playoffs, Super Bowl, Pro Bowl, and to repeat all of that the next year. He *hopes* his patient family will understand that during the season, football has a dominant place in his life.

Webster's New World College Dictionary defines *hope* as "a feeling that what is wanted is likely to happen; desire accompanied by expectation." It is also defined as a trust or reliance upon something. Many NFL or college players have come to realize that at the end of the day there is only one thing that warrants our expectations and will soothe our fears: a relationship with God Almighty. He is the only One who remains constant and the only One in whom we can place our complete trust. In the final analysis, He is our only Hope.

If you are discouraged, take heart. Look at the benefits that *hope* gives us:

- Hope gets us started in the right direction: *"But those who hope in the* LORD *will renew their strength. They will soar on wings like eagles; they will run and not grow weary, they will walk and not be faint" (Isaiah 40:31).*

- Hope helps us overcome obstacles: *"'For I know the plans I have for you,' declares the LORD, 'plans to prosper you and not to harm you, plans to give you hope and a future'"* (Jeremiah 29:11).

- Hope helps us keep going: *"Praise be to the God and Father of our Lord Jesus Christ! In his great mercy he has given us new birth into a living hope through the resurrection of Jesus Christ from the dead, and into an inheritance that can never perish, spoil or fade—kept in heaven for you"* (1 Peter 1:3–4).

Put your hope in God.
—PSALM 42:5

GAME PLAN:

1. Have you ever faced a time or situation when there seemed to be no hope? Look back through the promises of Isaiah 40:31, Jeremiah 29:11, and 1 Peter 1:3–4. Take heart—God will always give you hope when you lean on Him.

2. Spend time in the great outdoors to experience the peace and quiet needed to restore and renew your body, mind, and spirit. Let the hope of His creation relax and calm your spirit.

FOOTBALL HAS BEEN IN MY BLOOD EVER SINCE I WATCHED Y. A. TITTLE CHUCK A PASS TO HIS TIGHT END, Billy Wilson, back in the early 1950s. The passion, pageantry, and planning associated with this great sport all seem to resonate with my character.

As a young person, I would come home from church and immediately put on my football helmet and prepare for the TV game of the week. Because my father worked on Saturdays and got home late in the evenings, there really wasn't much time for us to throw the football around. Sunday's televised game was about the only time we were able to bond around something we both enjoyed. However, it was rare for me to sit through an entire game. My excitement spilled over to our long front yard, where I lived out all my fantasies about someday being an NFL player.

Our neighborhood was primarily made up of girls who were more interested in playing dolls than football. But I didn't let it bother me—even though there weren't a bunch of guys to play a pickup game, even though my front yard had cement walkways running through it, and even though I was not physically suited to play the game.

I would pretend to be an NFL quarterback, taking the ball from the center and then dropping back to bomb a pass as far and high as I could throw. This would give me time to race down to the end of the lawn to make a diving catch—sometimes landing on the lawn and sometimes on the walkways.

It had to look strange to anyone driving by the house to see this skinny young boy playing a one-man football game. The roles of quarterback and receiver were not enough—for who better to do the play-by-play announcing than the same person involved in the game? This would be done with all the sounds and words one could muster at eleven years of age. Then there were the imaginary tackles and kick returns and, of course, the victory

celebration after a score. Some days I would come in so exhausted that I would literally have to crawl into bed to recover.

This passion for the game carried over into high school, where my coach told me I was too skinny (5'11", 135 pounds) to play—without even checking my skill levels, he told me to go out for the golf team instead. Playing football in Oakland back in the early 1960s was nothing short of going into combat: most of the players were guys who'd flunked a grade or two and had full-grown physical maturity; they were big and strong and looking to intimidate any smaller player. Unfortunately, most formations called for two big tight ends and very quick running backs. I, of course, was neither big nor quick.

Utilizing an undersized flanker with good hands was something that hadn't yet reached the high school level; this left me to play off-season pick-up games with many of my varsity friends. When I finally got to college and could actually fill out a large jersey, the only option left was to play intramural sports. This was not really satisfying, because most players were neither committed nor passionate about the game. It usually ended up as a party scene with little room for developing game-winning strategies.

Having known and interviewed countless professional athletes, I find that those who've made it to the big leagues have four things in common:

1. God-given abilities: One thing that separates a college player from a high school player (and a pro player from a college player) is God-given ability.

2. Opportunity: The community in which you were raised, the schools you attended, and the coach's decisions to place you in a game at a certain time all factor into the opportunity to perform with the God-given abilities you have.

3. Commitment and dedication: Even the greats wouldn't have made it unless they daily worked at perfecting their skills. Practice is part of what separates the great ones from those who warm the bench.

4. Encouragement: I'm convinced that encouragement has to be the most important trait of all. You can lack a little in talent, you can play in a small unknown school, but you will most likely never develop the commitment and dedication you need without someone in the bleachers of your heart rooting you on and guiding you to the next opportunity.

I may have missed the opportunity to become a professional football player, but I didn't miss out on being drafted for the most important team—a team with a mission far greater than any NFL game. It's a team whose members are not always the most visible people on the field or the ones who look the best. They may even lack talent or physical ability. The unique thing about this team, though, is that it doesn't require a person to try out, and it costs nothing to join. The team is of divine inspiration; it's God's team—and it's the greatest team of all.

There is one thing lacking from God's football field—benches. Benches are for folks not playing the game—and when you're on God's team, you should always be in the game. When Jesus gave the Great Commission just before He left His disciples, He challenged them—and us—to join in the battle for souls (Matthew 28:18–20). Jesus' call isn't just a call to pastors or missionaries; it's a call to everyone who calls themselves *Christians*.

If you're not on His team, you need to be. Join today! We're always recruiting.

GAMEPLAN:

1. Are you an active player on God's team?

2. How do you keep in shape for the battles?

3. Are you an encourager to your teammates?

GOD'S GAME PLAN FOR LIFE

Like a head coach developing a good game plan for the Super Bowl, our heavenly Father developed a plan for our salvation. He initially hoped man would connect with Him through His great creation but Adam and Eve thought they had a better idea. Then God utilized great patriarchs like Moses and Joshua to present His plan to His chosen people (the Jews); then great kings, priests, judges, and prophets, only to be saddened with the condition of man's prideful spirit and sin-filled heart. So how does our Great Coach, God Almighty, get our attention? He sends in the best signal caller and the best sacrifice of all time: Jesus Christ.

The Romans Road lays out the only game plan for salvation through a series of Bible verses from the book of Romans. These verses form an easy-to-follow explanation of the message of salvation.

The Romans Road clearly defines:

1. who needs salvation,
2. why we need salvation,
3. how God provides salvation,
4. how we receive salvation,
5. the results of salvation, and
6. whether we go to heaven when we die.

For answers to these eternal questions and more, read the book of Romans found in the New Testament of your Bible.

If you believe the scriptures in Romans lead to the path of truth, you can respond by receiving God's free gift of salvation today. Here's how:

1. Admit you are a sinner.
2. Understand that as a sinner, you deserve death.
3. Believe Jesus Christ died on the cross to save you from sin and death. Believe that He conquered death itself when He rose from the grave.
4. Repent by turning from your old life of sin to a new life in Christ.
5. Receive, through faith in Jesus Christ, His free gift of salvation.

Additional Resources

For additional resources or assistance,
please call Men's Ministry Catalyst at 925-362-3340.
or e-mail us at lgfjim@frontier.com.
www.mensministrycatalyst.org

Endnotes

1. Lane Murphy, "RG3: Unforgettable," *Baylor Magazine*, Winter 2011–12.
2. "College Game Day Profiles Baylor QB Robert Griffin III: 'The Most Interesting Man in College Football,'" YouTube video, 2:03, posted October 1, 2011, http://espn.go.com/video/clip?id=704293.
3. "Robert Griffin III: 'My Relationship with God Is My Most Important Influence,'" YouTube video, 2:55, http://gospellightminute. wordpress.com/2012/05/06/robert-griffin-iii-my-relationship-with-god-is-my-most-important-influence/.
4. *Wikipedia*, "Jerry Rice," last modified November 2, 2012, http://en.wikipedia.org/wiki/Jerry_Rice.
5. "Frank Reich," *TheGoal.com*, accessed November 8, 2012, http://www.thegoal.com/players/football/reich_frank/reich_frank.html.
6. Charles R. Swindoll, "They, Being Dead, Still Speak: Hebrews 11:32–38" in "Character Counts: Building a Life That Pleases God," *Insight for Living*, 1988, http://www.insightforliving.com/pdf/retailseries/CharacterCounts_MessageMates.pdf.
7. Newspaper tribute to Tom Landry, *Dallas Star*, February 15, 2000, https://www.legacy.com/guestbooks/dfw/sponsor-guestbook.aspx?n=tom-landry&pid=139805600&cid=keep.
8. Gary Anderson, in discussion with the author.
9. H. D. M. Spence, The Pulpit Commentary: Ecclesiastes, vol. 21, (London: K. Paul, Trench, Tru?bner & Company, Limited, 1897), 50, http://books.google.com/books?id=s9EUAAAAYAAJ&pg=PA171&lpg=PA171&dq=%22The+beginnings+are+attended+with+anxieties+and+fears+as+to+ultimate+success%22&source=bl&ots=wy1F7gsPYo&sig=5GSVgioUEuXw4_IKYQVFZSLSKCg&hl=en#v=onepage&q=%22The%20beginnings%20are%20attended%20with%20anxieties%20and%20fears%20as%20to%20ultimate%20success%22&f=false.
10. Joe Gibbs, *Game Plan for Life: Your Personal Playbook for Success* (Carol Stream, IL: Tyndale, 2009).
11. Emmitt Smith, Hall of Fame speech (Canton, OH, August 7, 2010).
12. Emmitt Smith, interview by CBS-Dallas.
13. Steve Wilson, in discussion with the author.
14. Charles Swindoll, in a letter to Dan and Tom Grassi, April 1988.
15. Gene Getz, *The Measure of a Man: Twenty Attributes of a Godly Man* (Ventura, CA: Regal, 2004), 15–16.
16. Chris Berman, quoted in Terry Owens, *Super Bowl Marriage: From Training Camp to the Championship Game* (Random House Digital Inc., 2005).
17. Mike Waufle, in discussion with the author.
18. Bum Phillips, quoted in *San Francisco Chronicle*, December 1985.
19. Os Hillman, "The Power of the Tongue," *Marketplace Leaders*, June 9, 2012, http://www.marketplaceleaders.org/blog/power-ofthe-tongue/.
20. "Suicide: Facts at a Glance," Centers for Disease Control, Summer 2009, http://www.cdc.gov/violenceprevention/pdf/suicidedata-sheet-a.PDF.
21. Brian Goodell, quoted in Jane McManus, "Goodell Wants Longer NFL Season," *ESPNNewYork.com*, June 18, 2010, https://m.espn.go.com/general/story?storyId=5302244&lang=ES&wjb.
22. George W. Bush, Address to a Joint Session of Congress and the American People (Washington, DC: September 20, 2001), http://georgewbushwhitehouse.archives.gov/news/releases/2001/09/20010920-8.html.
23. "The Pleasure of a Year of Plenty," *Sports Illustrated*, September 9, 1968, http://sportsillustrated.cnn.com/vault/article/magazine/MAG1148024/25/index.htm.
24. Jone Johnson Lewis, "Marian Anderson Quotes," *About.com*, accessed November 8, 2012, http://womenshistory.about.com/od/quotes/a/marian_anderson.htm.
25. Jeff Sellers, "The Glory of the Ordinary," *Christianity Today*, January 8, 2001, http://www.christianitytoday.com/ct/2001/january8/7.60.html.
26. Sellers.
27. Sellers.
28. Sellers.
29. Sellers.
30. Sellers.
31. Sellers.
32. Larry Christenson, *The Renewed Mind: Becoming the Person God Wants You to Be* (Grand Rapids, MI: Bethany House, 2001), 105.
33. Dr. Larry Wilhite, in discussion with the author.
34. "Most pastors unsatisfied with personal prayer lives," *Baptist Press*, June 6, 2005, www.bpnews.net/bpnews.asp?id=20918.
35. Steve Wisniewski, in discussion with the author.
36. Steve Wisniewski, in discussion with the author.
37. Ollie Wright, "American football: Mike Singletary – 'Deep down every young man wants to be great,'" *The Independent*, July 31, 2010, http://www.independent.co.uk/sport/general/others/american-football-mike-singletary--deep-down-every-young-manwants-to-be-great-2039893.html.
38. Deion Sanders, *Power, Money & Sex: How Success Almost Ruined My Life* (Nashville, TN: Nelson/Word Publishing Group, 1999).
39. "Luigi Tarisio," *Wikipedia*, last modified October 27, 2012, http://en.wikipedia.org/wiki/Luigi_Tarisio.
40. Gary Swan, "Jones to Have Shoulder Surgery," *San Francisco Chronicle*, September 28, 1996, http://www.sfgate.com/sports/article/Jones-to-Have-Shoulder-Surgery-2965188.php.